Writing for Journalists

The new edition of *Writing for Journalists* focuses on the key issue for writers working across all forms of media today: how to produce clear, engaging and illuminating copy that will keep the reader hooked from start to finish.

Written by skilled specialist contributors and drawing on a broad range of examples to illustrate the best professional practice, this edition includes:

- chapters on how to write news, features and reviews whatever the format used for delivery
- expanded chapters on writing for digital publication in both shortform and longform
- top tips on writing columns and blogs from leading professionals
- an exploration of the importance of style and its impact on great journalistic writing
- an extensive glossary of terms used in journalism and suggestions for further reading.

This is an essential guide to good writing for all practising journalists and students of journalism.

Wynford Hicks is the author of various books on journalism and writing including *English for Journalists* (Routledge, 2013), now in its fourth edition, and *Quite Literally: Problem Words and How to Use Them* (Routledge, 2004).

Media Skills

EDITED BY RICHARD LANCE KEEBLE, LINCOLN UNIVERSITY

The *Media Skills* series provides a concise and thorough introduction to a rapidly changing media landscape. Each book is written by media and journalism lecturers or experienced professionals and is a key resource for a particular industry. Offering helpful advice and information and using practical examples from print, broadcast and digital media, as well as discussing ethical and regulatory issues, *Media Skills* books are essential guides for students and media professionals.

Writing for Journalists

THIRD EDITION

Wynford Hicks

with Sally Adams, Harriett Gilbert,
Tim Holmes and Jane Bentley

 Routledge
Taylor & Francis Group

LONDON AND NEW YORK

Third edition published 2016
by Routledge
2 Park Square, Milton Park, Abingdon, Oxon OX14 4RN

and by Routledge
711 Third Avenue, New York, NY 10017

Routledge is an imprint of the Taylor & Francis Group, an informa business

First published 1999 by Routledge

Second edition published 2008 by Routledge

British Library Cataloguing in Publication Data
A catalogue record for this book is available from the British Library

Library of Congress Cataloging in Publication Data
Hicks, Wynford, 1942–
    Writing for journalists / Wynford Hicks with Sally Adams, Harriett Gilbert,
    Tim Holmes and Jane Bentley.—Third edition.
        pages cm—(Media skills)
    Includes bibliographical references and index.
    1. Journalism—Authorship.   I. Adams, Sally, 1933–2014   II. Gilbert,
    Harriett, 1948–   III. Holmes, Tim, 1953–   IV. Bentley, Jane.   V. Title.
    PN4783.H53 2016
    808.06'607—dc23   2015031878

ISBN: 978-1-138-93209-8 (hbk)
ISBN: 978-1-138-93210-4 (pbk)
ISBN: 978-1-315-67944-0 (ebk)

Typeset in Goudy Old Style
by Keystroke, Station Road, Codsall, Wolverhampton

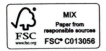

Printed and bound in Great Britain by
TJ International Ltd, Padstow, Cornwall

Contents

Contributors

Wynford Hicks has worked as a reporter, subeditor, feature writer, editor and editorial consultant for newspapers, books and magazines and as a teacher of journalism specialising in writing, subediting and the use of English. He is the author of *English for Journalists*, now in its fourth edition, *Quite Literally: Problem Words and How to Use Them*, and *The Basics of English Usage*.

Sally Adams, who died in 2014, was a writer, editor and lecturer. She was deputy editor of *She*, editor of *Mother and Baby* and *Weight Watchers Magazine*, a reporter on the *Christchurch Press*, New Zealand, and letters page editor on the *San Francisco Chronicle*. She wrote for the *Guardian*, *Daily Mail*, *Company*, *Evening Standard* and *Good Housekeeping* and was a visiting tutor at the London College of Fashion. She was the author of *Interviewing for Journalists*.

Harriett Gilbert is a broadcaster, journalist and novelist. She was literary editor of the *New Statesman* and has reviewed the arts for, among others, *Time Out*, the *Listener*, the *Independent* and the BBC. She presents *A Good Read* on BBC Radio 4 and *World Book Club* on BBC World Service Radio. She was for many years a senior lecturer in the Department of Journalism at City University London.

Tim Holmes is associate director of the Centre for Journalism Studies, Cardiff University, where he teaches and researches magazine journalism. His books include *The 21st Century Journalism Handbook*, *Magazine Journalism* and *Subediting and Production for Journalists*.

Jane Bentley is course director for Magazine Journalism at Cardiff University's Centre for Journalism Studies. She has previously worked as a magazine editor, managing editor, production editor and sub for a range of specialist consumer magazines covering cycling, tech, computing and video games.

Acknowledgements

The authors and publisher would like to thank all those journalists whose work we have quoted to illustrate the points made in this book. In particular we would like to thank the following for permission to reprint material:

'McDonald's the winner and loser'
Ian Cobain, *Daily Mail*, 20 June 1997 © *Daily Mail*

'Parsons' course record puts pressure on Woods'
Daily Telegraph, 14 February 1997 © *The Daily Telegraph*

'Man killed as L-drive car plunges off cliff'
Sean O'Neill, *Daily Telegraph*, 7 January 1998 © *The Daily Telegraph*
With thanks to Sean O'Neill

'Abbey overflows for Compton'
Matthew Engel, *The Guardian*, 2 July 1997. Copyright Guardian News & Media Ltd 2015

'Picnic in the bedroom'
Janet Harmer, *Caterer and Hotelkeeper* (now *The Caterer*), 11 June 1998. Reproduced with the permission of the Editor of *The Caterer*

'I love the job but do I have to wear that hat?'
Kerry Fowler, *Good Housekeeping*, June 1998. Reproduced with permission from *Good Housekeeping*, June 1998

Review of *The Whereabouts of Eneas McNulty*
Used with the permission of Adam Mars-Jones. Copyright Guardian News & Media Ltd 2015

Review of *From the Choirgirl Hotel*
Sylvia Patterson © Frank/Wagadon Ltd

Review of *Short Movie* by Laura Marling in *Uncut* by Laura Snapes © www.
timeincukcontent.com. Reproduced with the permission of Time Inc. UK

'The corrections column co-editor on the changing role of the subeditor'
Barbara Harper, theguardian.com, 27 May 2012. Copyright Guardian News &
Media Ltd 2015

'How to write journalism: Columns', Peter Cole, Michael White, *The Guardian*,
25 September 2008. Copyright Guardian News & Media Ltd 2015

Quotation from timeoutlondon Instagram post. Reproduced with permission of
Time Out

'10 most shared stories for November 2013', reproduced with permission of
NewsWhip.com

1

Introduction

What this book is

This book is about the craft of journalistic writing: putting one word after another so that the reader gets the message – or the joke – goes on reading and comes back for more. Good writing is essential to journalism: without it important news, intriguing stories, insight and analysis, gossip and opinion could not reach their potential audience.

Writing can also be a pleasure in itself: finding the right word, getting it to fit together with other words in a sentence, constructing a paragraph that conveys meaning and creates delight . . . There is pride in a well-written piece, in the positive feedback from editors, readers, fellow writers.

This book is a practical guide for those who write for publication in print or online, whether they are students, trainees or more experienced people, whether they work for a particular publication or as freelance contributors. Though aimed primarily at would-be and practising professionals it takes a broad rather than a narrow view of journalism. It recognises that a journalist today may well be a political activist, a sports fan or an academic, say, doing journalism in their spare time – probably not being paid for it – while a 'free-lance' is not necessarily someone who has chosen to be one.

We have revised and updated the book for this third edition. Inevitably the biggest changes are in the section covering digital publication where there are now separate chapters on shortform and longform writing. In general we have tried to concentrate our advice on online writing into these chapters rather than making frequent references to it in the rest of the book.

There is also a new – but very short – chapter on writing columns and blogs which recognises how the personal is a dominant theme in today's journalism. This is the argument of *Speaking Personally* by the ex-*Guardian* journalist Rosalind Coward. As she says, 'Thirty years ago the columns that existed were mainly addressing political, advice or lifestyle issues. Now there are columnists in every section of the newspaper.' Or as Andrew Marr, whom she quotes, puts it in *My Trade*, 'There are columns on gardens, cheap wine and etymology, columns on bicycling, on "my lovable children", on bird watching and sex with strangers, columns on every form of activity and dreaming known to mankind. There are ghosted columns by celebrities, and columns by celebrities that would have been much better if they had been ghosted.'

In revising the book we have kept most of the examples of good and bad practice that were included in previous editions: there seemed little point in replacing material that remains relevant.

What this book is not

This is neither a book about journalism nor a careers guide for would-be journalists. It does not set out to survey the field, to describe the various jobs that journalists do in different media. Nor is it a review of the issues in journalism. It does not discuss privacy or bias or the ownership of the press. It does not try to answer the question: is journalism in decline? Thus it is unlikely to be adopted as a media studies textbook.

It does not include broadcast journalism, though many of the points made also apply to TV and radio writing. It does not give detailed guidance on specialised areas such as sport, fashion, consumer and financial journalism. And it does not try to cover what might be called the public relations or propaganda sector of journalism, where getting a particular message across is the key. Magazines published by companies for their employees and customers, by charities for their donors and recipients, by trade unions and other organisations for their members – and all the other publications that are sponsored rather than market-driven – develop their own rules. Journalists who work in this sector learn to adapt to them.

Except in passing this book does not tell you how to find stories, do research or interview people. For detailed advice on interviewing see *Interviewing for Journalists*.

Though subeditors – and trainee subs – should find it useful as a guide to rewriting, it does not pretend to be a sub's manual. It does not tell you how to cut copy, write headlines or check proofs. It does not cover editing, design, media law . . .

We make no apology for this. In our view writing is the key journalistic skill without which everything else would collapse. That is why we think it deserves a book of its own.

Who cares about writing?

This may look like a silly question: surely all journalists, particularly editors, aspire to write well themselves and publish good writing? Alas, apparently not. The experience of some graduates of journalism courses in their first jobs is that much of what they learnt at college is neither valued nor even wanted by their editors and senior colleagues.

Of course, this might mean that what was being taught at college, instead of being proper journalism, was some kind of ivory-tower nonsense – but the evidence is all the other way. British journalism courses are responsive to industry demands and taught by journalists.

The problem is that many editors and senior journalists don't seem to bother very much about whether their publications are well written – or even whether they are in grammatically correct English. As Harry Blamires wrote in his introduction to *Correcting your English*, a collection of mistakes published in newspapers and magazines:

> Readers may be shocked, as indeed I was myself, to discover the sheer quantity of error in current journalism. They may be astonished to find how large is the proportion of error culled from the quality press and smart magazines. Assembling the bad sentences together en masse brings home to us that we have come to tolerate a shocking degree of slovenliness and illogicality at the level of what is supposed to be educated communication.

It's true that some of what Blamires calls 'error' is conscious colloquialism but most of his examples prove his point: many editors don't seem to bother very much about the quality of the writing they publish.

Others, on the other hand, do. There is some excellent writing published in British newspapers and periodicals. And it is clear that it can help to bring commercial success. For example, the *Daily Mail* outsells the *Daily Express*, its traditional rival, for all sorts of reasons. One of them certainly is the overall quality and professionalism of the *Mail's* writing.

But if you're a trainee journalist in an office where good writing is not valued, do not despair. Do the job you're doing as well as you can – and get ready for your next one. The future is more likely to be yours than your editor's.

Can writing be taught?

This is the wrong question – unless you're a prospective teacher of journalism. The question, if you're a would-be journalist (or indeed any kind of writer), is: can writing be learnt?

And the answer is: of course it can, providing that you have at least some talent and – what is more important – that you have a lot of determination and are prepared to work hard.

If you want to succeed as a writer, you must be prepared to read a lot, finding good models and learning from them; you must be prepared to think imaginatively about readers and how they think and feel rather than luxuriate inside your own comfortable world; you must be prepared to take time practising, experimenting, revising.

You must be prepared to listen to criticism and take it into account while not letting it get on top of you. You must develop confidence in your own ability but not let it become arrogance.

This book makes all sorts of recommendations about how to improve your writing but it cannot tell you how much progress you are likely to make. It tries to be helpful and encouraging but it does not pretend to be diagnostic. And – unlike those gimmicky writing courses advertised to trap the vain, the naive and the unwary – it cannot honestly 'guarantee success or your money back'.

Getting down to it

Make a plan before you start

Making a plan before you start to write is an excellent idea, even if you keep it in your head. And the longer and more complex the piece, the more there is to be gained from setting the plan down on paper – or on the keyboard.

Of course you may well revise the plan as you go, particularly if you start writing before your research is completed. But that is not a reason for doing without a plan.

Write straight onto the keyboard

Unless you want to spend your whole life writing, which won't give you much time to find and research stories – never mind going to the pub or practising the cello – don't bother with a handwritten draft. Why introduce an unnecessary stage into the writing process?

Don't use the excuse that your typing is slow and inaccurate. First, obviously, learn to touch-type, so you can write straight onto the keyboard at the speed at which you think. For most people this will be about 25 words per minute (wpm) – a speed far slower than that of a professional copy typist.

(There's a key distinction here between the skills of typing and shorthand. As far as writing is concerned, there's not much point in learning to type faster than 25wpm: accuracy is what counts. By contrast, the shorthand speeds that most journalism students and trainees reach if they work hard, typically 80–100wpm, are of limited use in getting down extensive quotes of normal speech. Shorthand really comes into its own above 100wpm.)

Even if you don't type very well, you should avoid the handwritten draft stage. After all, the piece is going to end up typed – presumably by you. So get down to it straightaway, however few fingers you use.

Write notes to get started

Some people find the act of writing difficult. They feel inhibited from starting to write, as though they were on a high diving board or at the top of a ski run.

Reporters don't often suffer from this kind of writer's block because, assuming they have found a story in the first place, the task of writing an intro for it is usually a relatively simple one. Note: not easy but simple, meaning that reporters have a limited range of options; they are not conventionally expected to invent, to be 'creative'.

One reason why journalists should start as reporters is that it's a great way to get into the habit of writing.

However, if you've not yet acquired the habit and tend to freeze at the keyboard, don't just sit there agonising. Having written your basic plan, add further headings, enumerate, list, illustrate. Don't sweat over the first paragraph: begin somewhere in the middle; begin with something you know you're going to include, like an anecdote or a quote. You can reposition it later. Get started, knowing that on the keyboard you're not committed to your first draft.

Revise, revise

Always leave yourself time to revise what you have written. Even if you're writing news to a tight deadline, try to spend a minute or two looking over your story. And if you're a feature writer or reviewer, revision is an essential part of the writing process.

If you're lucky, a competent subeditor will check your copy before it goes to press, but that is no reason to pretend to yourself that you are not responsible for what you write. As well as looking for the obvious – errors of fact, names wrong, spelling and grammar mistakes, confusion caused by bad punctuation – try to read your story from the reader's point of view. Does it make sense in their terms? Is it clear? Does it really hit the target?

Master the basics

You can't start to write well without having a grasp of the basics of English usage such as grammar, spelling and punctuation. To develop a journalistic style you will need to learn how to use quotes, handle reported speech, choose the right word from a variety of different ones. When should you use foreign words and phrases, slang, jargon – and what about clichés? What is 'house style'? And so on.

The basics of English and journalistic language are covered in a companion volume, *English for Journalists*. In this book we have in general tried not to repeat material included there.

Different kinds of print journalism

There are obviously different kinds of print journalism – and thus different demands on the journalist as writer. Conventionally, people distinguish in market-sector terms between newspapers and periodicals, between upmarket (previously 'broadsheet') and downmarket (previously 'tabloid') papers, between consumer and business-to-business (from now on in this book called 'b2b') periodicals, and so on.

Some of these conventional assumptions can be simplistic when applied to the way journalism is written. For example, a weekly b2b periodical is in fact a newspaper. In its approach to news writing it has as much in common with other weeklies – local newspapers, say, or Sunday newspapers – as it does with monthly b2b periodicals. Indeed 'news' in monthly publications is not the same thing at all.

Second, while everybody goes on about the stylistic differences between the top and bottom ends of the newspaper market, less attention is paid to those between mid-market tabloids, such as the *Mail*, and the redtops, such as the *Sun*. Whereas features published by the *Guardian* are occasionally reprinted by the *Mail* (and vice versa) with no alterations to the text, most *Mail* features would not fit easily into the *Sun*.

Third, in style terms there are surprising affinities that cross the conventional divisions. For example, the *Sun* and the *Guardian* both include more jokes in the text and more punning headlines than the *Mail* does. Fourth, while *Guardian* stories typically have longer words, sentences and paragraphs than those in the *Mail*, which are in turn longer than those in the *Sun*, it does not follow, for example, that students and trainees who want to end up at the *Guardian* should practise writing long words and sentences.

Indeed our advice to students and trainees is not to begin by imitating the style of a particular publication – or even a particular type of publication. Instead we think you should try to develop an effective writing style by learning from the various good models available. We think that – whoever you are – you can learn from good newspapers and periodicals, whether upmarket or downmarket, daily, weekly or monthly.

This book does not claim to give detailed guidance on all the possible permutations of journalistic writing. Instead we take the old-fashioned view that journalism students and trainees should gain a basic all-round competence in news and feature writing.

Thus we cover the straight news story and a number of variations, but not foreign news as such, since trainees are unlikely to find themselves being sent to a war zone. Also, as has already been said, we do not set out to give detailed guidance on specialist areas such as financial and sports reporting. In features we concentrate on the basic formats used in newspapers, consumer magazines and the b2b press.

We also include a chapter on reviewing because it is not a branch of feature writing but a separate skill which is in great demand. Reviews are written by all sorts of journalists including juniors and 'experts' who often start with little experience of writing for publication.

We have taken examples from a wide range of publications and websites but we repeat: our intention is not to 'cover the field of journalism'. In newspapers we have often used examples from the nationals rather than regional or local papers because they are more familiar to readers and in periodicals, too, we have tended to use the bigger, better-known titles.

Style

In the chapters that follow the different demands of writing news, features and reviews – and writing online – are discussed separately. In the final chapter we look at style as such. We review what the experts have said about the principles of good journalistic writing and suggest how you can develop an effective style.

For whatever divides the different forms of journalism there is such a thing as a distinctive journalistic approach to writing. Journalism – at least in the Anglo-Saxon tradition – is informal rather than formal; active rather than passive; a temporary, inconclusive, ad hoc, interim reaction rather than a definitive, measured statement.

Journalists always claim to deliver the latest – but never claim to have said or written the last word.

Journalism may be factual or polemical, universal or personal, laconic or ornate, serious or comic, but on top of the obvious mix of information and entertainment its stock-in-trade is shock, surprise, contrast. That is why journalists are always saying 'BUT', often for emphasis at the beginning of sentences.

All journalists tell stories, whether interesting in themselves or used to grab the reader's attention or illustrate a point. Journalists usually prefer analogy (finding a similar example of something) to analysis (breaking something down to examine it).

Journalists – in print as well as broadcasting – use the spoken word all the time. They quote what people say to add strength and colour to observation and they often use speech patterns and idioms in their writing.

Journalists are interpreters between specialist sources and the general public, translators of scientific jargon into plain English, scourges of obfuscation, mystification, misinformation. Or they should be.

A good journalist can always write a story short even if they would prefer to have the space for an expanded version. Thus the best general writing exercise for a would-be journalist is what English teachers call the precis or summary, in which a prose passage is reduced to a prescribed length. Unlike the simplest form of subediting, in which whole paragraphs are cut from a story so that its style remains unaltered, the precis involves condensing and rewriting as well as cutting.

Journalists have a confused and ambivalent relationship with up-to-date slang, coinages, trendy expressions. They are always looking for new, arresting ways of saying the same old things – but they do more than anybody else to ensure that the new quickly becomes the familiar. Thus good journalists are always trying (and often failing) to avoid clichés.

Politicians, academics and other people who take themselves far too seriously sometimes criticise journalism for being superficial. In other words, they seem to be saying, without being deep it is readable. From the writing point of view this suggests that it has hit the target.

2
Writing news

What is news?

News is easy enough to define. To be news, something must be factual, new and interesting.

There must be facts to report – without them there can be no news. The facts must be new – to your readers at least. And these facts must be likely to interest your readers.

So if a historian makes a discovery about the eating habits of the ancient Britons, say, somebody can write a news story about it for the periodical *History Today*. The information will be new to its readers, though the people concerned lived hundreds or thousands of years ago. Then, when the story is published, it can be followed up by a national newspaper like the *Daily Telegraph* or the *Sunday Mirror*, on the assumption that it would appeal to their readers.

Being able to identify what will interest readers is called having a news sense. There are all sorts of dictums about news (some of which contradict others): that bad news sells more papers than good news; that news is what somebody wants to suppress; that readers are most interested in events and issues that affect them directly; that news is essentially about people; that readers want to read about people like themselves; that readers are, above all, fascinated by the lives, loves and scandals of the famous . . .

It may sound cynical but the most useful guidance for journalism students and trainees is that news is what's now being published in print news outlets and online. In other words, whatever the guides and textbooks may say, what the papers actually say is more important.

Some commentators have distinguished between 'hard' news about 'real', 'serious', 'important' events affecting people's lives and 'soft' news about 'trivial' incidents (such as a cat getting stuck up a tree and being rescued by the fire brigade). Those analysing the content of newspapers for its own sake may find this distinction useful, but in terms of journalistic style it can be a dead end. The fact is that there is no clear stylistic distinction between 'hard' and 'soft' news writing.

It makes more sense to say that there is a mainstream, traditional approach to news writing – with a number of variants. The reporter may use one of these variants – the narrative style, say – to cover the rescue of a cat stuck up a tree or an exchange of fire in Afghanistan. Or they may decide, in either case, to opt for the traditional approach. In fact both 'hard' and 'soft' news can be written either way.

Since we're talking definitions, why is a news report called a 'story'? Elsewhere, the word means anecdote or narrative, fiction or fib – though only a cynic would say that the last two definitions tell the essential truth about journalism.

In fact the word 'story' applied to a news report emphasises that it is a construct, something crafted to interest a reader (rather than an unstructured 'objective' version of the facts). In some ways the word is misleading since, as we shall see, a traditional news story does not use the narrative style.

And, while we're at it, what is an 'angle'? As with 'story' the dictionary seems to provide ammunition for those hostile to journalism. An angle is 'a point of view, a way of looking at something (*informal*); a scheme, a plan devised for profit (*slang*)', while to angle is 'to present (news, etc) in such a way as to serve a particular end' (*Chambers Dictionary*, 10th edition, 2006).

We can't blame the dictionary for jumbling things together but there is a key distinction to be made between having a way of looking at something (essential if sense is to be made of it) and presenting news to serve a particular purpose (propaganda). Essentially, a news angle comes from the reporter's interpretation of events – which they invite the reader to share.

> McDonald's won a hollow victory over two Green campaigners yesterday after the longest libel trial in history.
> *Daily Mail*

The word 'hollow', particularly combined with 'longest', shows that the reporter has a clear idea of what the story is. Advocates of 'objective' journalism may criticise this 'reporting from a point of view' – but nowadays all national papers do it.

> Victims of the world's worst *E coli* food poisoning outbreak reacted furiously last night after the Scottish butcher's shop which sold contaminated meat was fined just £2,250.
> *Guardian*

That 'just' shows clearly what the reporter thinks of the fine.

A quick word before you start

It's not original to point out that news journalism is all about questions: the ones you ask yourself before you leave the office or pick up the phone; the ones you ask when you're interviewing and gathering material – above all, the ones your reader wants you to answer.

Begin with the readers of your publication. You need to know who they are, what they're interested in, what makes them tick. (For more on this see 'Writing features', page 41.)

Then what's the story about? In some cases – a fire, say – the question answers itself. In others – a complicated fraud case – you may have to wrestle with the material to make it make sense.

Never be afraid to ask the news editor or a senior colleague if you're confused about what you're trying to find out. Better a moment's embarrassment before you start than the humiliation of realising, after you've written your story, that you've been missing the point all along. The same applies when you're interviewing. Never be afraid to ask apparently obvious questions – if you have to.

The trick, though, is to be well briefed – and then ask your questions. Try to know more than a reporter would be expected to know. But don't parade your knowledge: ask your questions in a straightforward way. Challenge when necessary, probe certainly, interrupt if you have to – but never argue when you're interviewing. Be polite, firm, controlled, professional. It may sound old-fashioned but you represent your publication and its readers.

Routine is vital to news gathering. Always read your own publication – and its rivals – regularly; maintain your contacts file and diary; remember to ask people their ages if that is what the news editor insists on. Above all, when interviewing, get people's names right. Factual accuracy is vital to credible news journalism. A bright and clever story is worse than useless if its content is untrue: more people will read it – and more people will be misinformed.

News formulas

The two most commonly quoted formulas in the traditional approach to news writing are Rudyard Kipling's six questions (sometimes abbreviated to the five Ws) and the news pyramid (usually described as 'inverted').

The six questions

Kipling's six questions – who, what, how, where, when, why – provide a useful checklist for news stories, and it's certainly possible to write an intro that includes them all. The textbook example is:

> Lady Godiva (WHO) rode (WHAT) naked (HOW) through the streets of Coventry (WHERE) yesterday (WHEN) in a bid to cut taxes (WHY).

This is facetiously called the clothesline intro – because you can hang everything on it. There is nothing wrong with this particular example but there is no reason why every news intro should be modelled on it. Indeed some intros would become very unwieldy if they tried to answer all six questions.

In general, the six questions should all be answered somewhere in the story – but there are exceptions. For example, in a daily paper a reporter may have uncovered a story several days late. They will try to support it with quotes obtained 'yesterday'; but there is no point in emphasising to readers that they are getting the story late. So the exact date on which an event took place should not be given unless it is relevant.

In weekly papers and periodicals 'this week' may be relevant; 'last week' as a regular substitute for the daily paper's 'yesterday' is usually pointless. Even worse is 'recently', which carries a strong whiff of staleness and amateurism – best left to the club newsletter and the parish magazine.

So the six questions should be kept as a checklist. When you've written a news story, check whether you've failed to answer one of the questions – and so weakened your story. But if there is no point in answering a particular question, don't bother with it.

Two of these questions – who and what – are obviously essential. In all news intros somebody or something must do or experience something. A useful distinction can be made between 'who' stories, in which the focus is on the person concerned, and 'what' stories, which are dominated by what happens. As we shall see, drawing this distinction can help you decide whether or not to include a person's name in an intro.

The news pyramid

This particular pyramid is not quite as old as the ancient Egyptians. But as a formula for analysing and practising news writing it goes back a long way. And the pyramid is certainly a useful idea (the only mystery is why most commentators insist on 'inverting' it – turning it upside down – when it does the job perfectly well the right way up).

The purpose of the pyramid is to show that the points in a news story are made in descending order of importance. News is written so that readers can stop reading when they have satisfied their curiosity – without worrying that something important is being held back. To put it another way, news is written so that subeditors can cut stories from the bottom up – again, without losing something important.

As we shall see, some stories don't fit the pyramid idea as well as others – but it remains a useful starting point for news writing.

Intros 1: traditional

The news intro should be able to stand on its own. Usually one sentence, it conveys the essence of the story in a clear, concise, punchy way: general enough to be understood; precise enough to be distinguished from other stories.

It should contain few words – usually fewer than 30, often fewer than 20.

First, decide what your story is about: like any other sentence a news intro has a subject. Then ask yourself two questions: why this story now? And how would you start telling your reader the story if you met them in the pub?

The intro is your chance to grab your reader's attention so that they read the story. If you fail, the whole lot goes straight in the bin.

The intro should make sense instantly to your reader. Often it should say how the story will affect them, what it means in practice. And always prefer the concrete to the abstract.

- Don't start with questions or with things that need to be explained – direct quotes, pronouns, abbreviations (except the most common).
- Don't start with things that create typographical problems – figures, italics, direct quotes again.
- Don't start with things that slow the sentence – subordinate clauses, participles, parentheses, long, difficult, foreign words.
- Don't start with when and where, how and why.
- Do start with a crisp sentence in clear English that tells the story.

When you've finished writing, go back and polish your intro; then see if you can use it to write a working news headline. That will tell you whether you've still got more work to do.

Who or what?

If everybody were equal in news terms, all intros might be general and start: 'A man', 'A company', 'A football team'. Alternatively, they might all be specific and start: 'Michael Gove'/'John Evans'; 'JCB'/'Evans Hairdressing'; 'Arsenal'/'Brize Norton Rangers'.

Between 'A man' and 'Michael Gove'/'John Evans' there are various steps, for example 'A Tory politician'/'An Islington hairdresser'. Then there's the explaining prefix that works as a title: 'Justice secretary Michael Gove'/ 'Islington hairdresser John Evans' (though some upmarket papers still refuse to use this snappy 'tabloid' device).

But the point is that people are not equally interesting in news terms. Some are so well known that their name is enough to sell a story, however trivial. Others will only get into the paper by winning the national lottery or dying in a car crash.

Here is a typical WHO intro about a celebrity – without his name there would be no national paper story:

> Comic Eddie Izzard fought back when he was attacked in the street by an
> abusive drunk, a court heard yesterday.
> *Daily Mail*

Note the contrast with:

> A crown court judge who crashed his Range Rover while five times over
> the drink-drive limit was jailed for five months yesterday.
> *Daily Telegraph*

A crown court judge he may be – but not many *Telegraph* readers would recognise his name: it is his occupation not his name that makes this a front-page story.

And finally the anonymous figure 'A man' – his moment of infamy is entirely due to what he has done:

> A man acquitted of murder was convicted yesterday of harassing the family
> of a police officer who helped investigate him.
> *Guardian*

So the first question to ask yourself in writing an intro is whether your story is essentially WHO or WHAT: is the focus on the person or on what they've done? This helps to answer the question: does the person's name go in the intro or is their identification delayed to the second or third par?

Local papers tend to have stories about 'an Islington man' where the nationals prefer 'a hairdresser' and b2b papers go straight to 'top stylist John Evans'. On the sports page both locals and nationals use 'Arsenal' and their nickname 'the Gunners' (or 'Gooners'). In their own local paper Brize Norton Rangers may be 'Rangers'; but when they play Arsenal in the FA Cup, to everybody else they have to become something like 'the non-League club Brize Norton' or 'non-Leaguers Brize Norton'.

When?

There is an exception to the general rule that you shouldn't begin by answering the WHEN question:

> Two years after merchant bank Barings collapsed with £830m losses, it is back in hot water.
> *Daily Mail*

If starting this way gives the story a strong angle, by all means do it. (And the same argument could apply to WHERE, HOW and WHY – but such occasions are rare.)

After

'After' is a useful way of linking two stages of a story without having to say 'because'. Always use 'after' rather than 'following' to do this: it is shorter, clearer – and not journalistic jargon.

> A Cambridge student who killed two friends in a drunken car crash left court a free man yesterday after a plea for clemency from one of the victims' parents.
> *Guardian*

In this case the judge may have been influenced by the plea for clemency – but even if he was, that would still not enable the reporter to say 'because'.

> A woman artist was on the run last night after threatening to shoot three judges in the Royal Courts of Justice.
> *Daily Mail*

Here the first part of the intro is an update on the second.

In some stories the 'after' links the problem with its solution:

> A six-year-old boy was rescued by firemen after he became wedged under a portable building being used as a polling station.
> *Daily Telegraph*

In others the 'after' helps to explain the first part of the intro:

> An aboriginal man was yesterday speared 14 times in the legs and beaten on the head with a nulla nulla war club in a traditional punishment after Australia's courts agreed to recognise tribal justice.
> *Guardian*

Sometimes 'after' seems too weak to connect the two parts of an intro:

> Examiners were accused of imposing a 'tax on Classics' yesterday after announcing they would charge sixth formers extra to take A-levels in Latin and Greek.
> *Daily Mail*

It is certainly true that A happened after B – but it also happened because of B. There should be a stronger link between the two parts of the intro.

One point or two?

As far as possible, intros should be about one point not two, and certainly not several. The double intro can sometimes work:

> Bill Clinton has completed his selection of the most diverse Cabinet in US history by appointing the country's first woman law chief.
>
> The President-elect also picked a fourth black and a second Hispanic to join his top team.
> *Daily Mail*

Here the *Mail* reporter (or sub) has divided the intro into two separate pars. It's easier to read this way.

> Australian Lucas Parsons equalled the course record with a nine-under-par 64, but still could not quite take the spotlight away from Tiger Woods in the first round of the Australian Masters in Melbourne yesterday.
> *Daily Telegraph*

Yes, it's a bit long but the reporter just gets away with it. Everybody is expecting to read about current hero Tiger Woods but here's this sensation – a course record by a little-known golfer.

In some stories the link between two points is so obvious that a concise double intro is probably the only way to go. In the two examples below 'both' makes the point:

> Battersea's boxing brothers Howard and Gilbert Eastman both maintained their undefeated professional records at the Elephant and Castle Leisure Centre last Saturday.
> *Wandsworth Borough Guardian*

> Queens Park Rangers and Sheffield United both announced full-year operating losses.
> *Guardian*

(Obvious or not, the link does give problems in developing the story – see 'Splitting the pyramid', page 30.)

The main cause of clutter in news stories is trying to say too much in the intro. This makes the intro itself hard to read – and the story hard to develop clearly. Here is a cluttered intro:

> Marketing junk food to children has to become socially unacceptable, a leading obesity expert will say today, warning that the food industry has done too little voluntarily to help avert what a major report this week will show is a 'far worse scenario than even our gloomiest predictions'.
> Guardian

The problem here is that the reporter wants to link two apparently unconnected statements on the same subject – which is fair enough in the story but certainly not in the intro where it can only confuse. The natural place to end the intro is after 'will say today'. That would leave it clear and concise.

Instead the sentence meanders on with the 'warning' followed by the doom-laden 'major report'. But what's being asserted is not 'warning' at all – 'warning' here is journalese for saying/claiming etc. Then there's the word 'voluntarily' – which adds nothing to 'done too little'; there's 'help' – which is unnecessary; there's 'major' – journalese again (whoever heard of a 'minor' report?); and there's the word 'show', which implies endorsement of the report's findings instead of merely describing them. Finally we get to the 'scenario' and the gloomy predictions.

A sentence that starts with a simple message in clear ordinary language – 'stop marketing junk food to children' – degenerates into clumsily expressed, convoluted jargon.

As and when

'As' is often used in intros to link two events that occur at the same time:

> A National Lottery millionaire was planning a lavish rerun of her wedding last night as a former colleague claimed she was being denied her rightful share of the jackpot.
> Daily Telegraph

This approach rarely works. Here the main point of the story is not A (the planned second wedding) but B (the dispute) – as is shown by the fact that the next ten pars develop it; the eleventh par covers the wedding plans; and the final four pars return to the dispute.

In contrast to 'as', 'when' is often used for intros that have two bites at the cherry: the first grabs the reader's attention; the second justifies the excitement:

A crazed woman sparked panic in the High Court yesterday when she burst in and held a gun to a judge's head.
Sun

A naive Oxford undergraduate earned a double first from the university of life when he was robbed by two women in one day, a court heard today.
London *Evening Standard*

Specific or summary?

Should an intro begin with an example, then generalise – or make a general statement, then give an example? Should it be specific – or summary portmanteau/comprehensive?

Torrential rain in Spain fell mainly on the lettuces last month – and it sent their prices rocketing.
Guardian

This intro to a story on retail price inflation grabs the attention in a way that a general statement would not. Whenever possible, choose a specific news point rather than a general statement for your intro.

But weather reports can be exceptions. Here's the first par of a winter weather story:

The first snowfalls of winter brought much of the South East to a standstill today after temperatures plunged below freezing. The wintry onslaught claimed its first victim when a motorist was killed in Kent.
London *Evening Standard*

Pity about 'plunged' and 'wintry onslaught' – they were probably in the cuttings for last year's snow story too. But otherwise the intro works well for the *Standard*, which covers much of the south east around London. A Kent paper would have led on the death.

The wider the area your paper covers the greater the argument for a general intro on a weather story.

Fact or claim?

This is a vital distinction in news. Are you reporting something as fact – or reporting that somebody has said something in a speech or a written report? An avalanche of news comes by way of reports and surveys; courts, councils and tribunals; public meetings and conferences.

In these stories you must attribute – say who said it – in the intro. Tabloids sometimes delay the attribution to the second or third par – but this practice is not recommended: it risks confusion in the reader's mind.

> Skiers jetting off for the slopes are risking a danger much worse than broken bones, according to university research published today.
> Guardian

Note that this is a general not a detailed attribution – that comes later in the story. Only give a name in the intro when it is likely to be recognised by the reader.

The WHO/WHAT distinction is important in these stories. The rule is to start with what is said – unless the person saying it is well known, as in:

> Sir Jackie Stewart, the former motor-racing world champion, has accused his fellow Scots of being lazy and overdependent on public sector 'jobs for life'.
> Sunday Times

If your story is based on a speech or written report you give the detail (eg WHERE) lower in the story. But if it is based on a press conference or routine interview, there is no need to mention this. Writing 'said at a press conference' or 'said in a telephone interview' is like nudging the reader and saying 'I'm a journalist, really'.

Some publications, particularly b2b periodicals, are inclined to parade the fact that they have actually interviewed somebody for a particular news story, as in 'told the *Muckshifters' Gazette*'. This is bad style because it suggests that on other occasions no interview has taken place – that the publication's news stories are routinely based on unchecked press releases. Where this is standard practice, it is stretching a point to call it 'news writing'.

Past, present – or future?

Most news intros report what happened, so are written in the past tense. But some are written in the present tense, which is more immediate, more vivid to the reader:

> An advert for Accurist watches featuring an ultra-thin model is being investigated by the Advertising Standards Authority.
> Guardian

News of the investigation makes a better intro than the fact that people have complained to the ASA: as well as being more immediate it takes the story a stage further.

Some intros combine the present tense for the latest stage in the story with the past tense for the facts that grab the attention:

> BT is tightening up its telephone security system after its confidential list of ex-directory numbers was penetrated – by a woman from Ruislip.
> Observer

This intro also illustrates two other points: the use of 'After' to link two stages of a story (see page 15) and 'The element of surprise' (see page 21). The dash emphasises the point that this huge and powerful organisation was apparently outwitted by a mere individual.

Speech-report intros are often written with the first part in the present tense and the main verb of the second part in the past tense:

> Copyright is freelances' work and they must never give it away, said Carol Lee, who is coordinating the NUJ campaign against the *Guardian's* new rights offensive.
> Journalist

Note that the first part of the intro is not a quote. Quotes are not used in good news intros for two main reasons: as Harold Evans noted back in 1972,

> Offices where intros are still set with drop caps usually ban quote intros because of the typographical complications. There is more against them than that. The reader has to do too much work. He has to find out who is speaking and he may prefer to move on.

Drop caps in news intros (and male pronouns) aren't as common as they were – but the rule holds good: don't make the reader do too much work. When you write the intro for a speech report, take the speaker's main point and, if necessary, put it in your own words. Thus the version you end up with may or may not be the actual words of the speaker. In this example we don't know what Carol Lee's words were – but they could have been more elaborate.

Here, the editing process could have gone further. A more concise version of the intro would be:

> Freelances must never give up copyright, said Carol Lee . . .

Some present-tense intros look forward to the future:

> Yule Catto, the chemicals group, is believed to be preparing a £250m bid for Holliday Chemical, its sector rival.
> *Sunday Times*

And some intros are actually written in the future tense:

> More than 1,000 travel agency shops will unite this week to become the UK's largest high street package holiday chain, using the new name Worldchoice.
> *Observer*

Where possible, use the present or the future tense rather than the past and, if you're making a prediction, be as definite as you can safely be.

The element of surprise

> A woman who fell ill with a collapsed lung on a Boeing 747 had her life saved by two doctors who carried out an operation with a coathanger, a bottle of mineral water, brandy and a knife and fork.
> *Guardian*

> Two British doctors carried out a life-saving operation aboard a jumbo jet – with a coat hanger.
> *Daily Mail*

> A doctor saved a mum's life in a mid-air operation – using a coathanger, pen top, brandy and half a plastic bottle.
> *Sun*

These three intros agree with one another more than they disagree: a woman's life was saved in mid-air by doctors using what lay to hand including a coat hanger.

The best way of writing the intro puts the human drama first but does not leave the intriguing aspect of the means used until later in the story. That would risk the reader saying 'Good but so what?' – and going on to something else.

Nor in this kind of story should you begin with the bizarre. 'A coat hanger, pen top, brandy and half a plastic bottle were used in an emergency midair operation . . .' misplaces the emphasis. In any newspaper the fact that a woman's life was saved comes first.

The three intros quoted above show various strengths and weaknesses: the *Guardian*'s is longwinded and clumsy, though accurate and informative; the *Mail*'s is concise, but is 'a jumbo jet' better than 'a Boeing 747' (in the intro who cares what make of plane it was?) and why just a coat hanger – what happened to the brandy? The *Sun* spares us the planespotter details but insists on calling the woman 'a mum' (while failing to mention her children anywhere in the story).

And is the story mainly about a woman (*Guardian*), a doctor (*Sun*) or two British doctors (*Mail*)?

But in style the biggest contrast here is between the approach of the *Mail* and the *Sun* which both signal the move from human drama to bizarre detail by using the dash – and that of the *Guardian* which does not.

When you start with an important fact, then want to stress an unusual or surprising aspect of the story in the same sentence, the natural way to do this is with the dash. It corresponds exactly with the way you would pause and change your tone of voice in telling the story.

The running story

When a story runs from day to day it would irritate the reader to keep talking about 'A man' in the intro. Also it would be pointless: most readers either read the paper regularly or follow the news in some other way. But it is essential that each news story as a whole should include necessary background for new readers.

> The tiger which bit a circus worker's arm off was the star of the famous Esso TV commercial.
> London *Evening Standard*

After this intro the story gives an update on the victim's condition and repeats details of the accident.

Court reports are often running stories. Here the trick is to write an intro that works for both sets of readers: it should be both vivid and informative.

> The 10-year-old girl alleged to have been raped by classmates in a primary school toilet said yesterday that she just wanted to be a 'normal kid'.
> *Guardian*

In some cases phrases like 'renewed calls' or 'a second death' make the point that this is one more stage in a continuing drama:

> Another Catholic man was shot dead in Belfast last night just as the IRA issued a warning that the peace process in Northern Ireland was on borrowed time.
> *Guardian*

The follow-up

Like the running story, the follow-up should not start 'A man' if the original story is likely to be remembered. In the following example the 'mystery businessman' has enjoyed a second expensive meal weeks after the first – but the story is his identity. His name is given in par three.

> The mystery businessman who spent more than £13,000 on a dinner for three in London is a 34-year-old Czech financier who manages a £300m fortune.
> *Sunday Times*

Intros 2: variation

The possible variations are endless: any feature-writing technique can be applied to news writing – if it works. But two variations are particularly common: selling the story and the narrative style. The narrative sometimes turns into the delayed drop (see page 24).

Selling the story

Here a selling intro is put in front of a straight news story:

> If you have friends or relations in High Street banking, tell them – warn them – to find another job. Within five years, the Internet is going to turn their world upside down.
>
> This is the confident forecast in a 200-page report . . .
> *Daily Mail*

The report's forecast is that the internet will turn the world of banking upside down – that is where the straight news story starts. But the *Mail* reporter has added an intro that dramatises the story and says what it will mean in practice – for people like the reader.

> They were the jeans that launched (or relaunched) a dozen pop songs.
>
> Now Levis, the clothing manufacturer that used to turn everything it touched into gold, or even platinum, has fallen on harder times.
>
> Yesterday the company announced that it is to cut its North American workforce by a third.
> *Guardian*

The straight news in par three follows an intro that gives the story a nostalgic flavour: the reader is brought into it and reminded of their pleasurable past buying jeans and listening to pop music.

The risk with this kind of selling intro is that some readers may be turned off by it: they may not have friends in retail banking; they may not feel nostalgic about jeans and pop music. What is important here is knowing your readers and how they are likely to react.

The narrative style

Here the traditional news story approach gives way to the kind of narrative technique used in fiction:

> The thud of something falling to the ground stopped Paul Hallett in his tracks as he tore apart the rafters of an old outside lavatory.
>
> The handyman brushed off his hands and picked up a dusty wallet, half expecting to find nothing inside.

But picking through the contents one by one, Mr Hallett realised he had stumbled upon the details of a US Air Force chaplain stationed at a nearby RAF base in Suffolk 50 years earlier.
Daily Mail

Choral scholar Gavin Rogers-Ball was dying for a cigarette. Stuck on a coach bringing the Wells Cathedral choir back from a performance in Germany, he had an idea – ask one of the boys to be sick and the adult members of the choir could step off the bus for a smoke.

It was a ruse that was to cost the alto dear . . .
Guardian

Both stories begin with a dramatic moment – and name their main character. As with fiction the trick is to get the reader involved with that person and what happens to them.

News stories about court cases and tribunals can often be handled in this way, and so can any light or humorous subject. But for the technique to work there must be a story worth telling.

If you can, try to avoid the awkward use of variation words to describe your main character. 'Alto' in the *Guardian* story is particularly clumsy. (See 'Variation' on page 34.)

The delayed drop

Here the story is written in narrative style and what would be the first point in a conventional intro – the real news, if you like – is kept back for effect. The change of direction is sometimes signalled by a 'BUT':

A pint-sized Dirty Harry, aged 11, terrorised a school when he pulled out a Magnum revolver in the playground. Screaming children fled in panic as the boy, who could hardly hold the powerful handgun, pointed it at a teacher.

But headmaster Arthur Casson grabbed the boy and discovered that the gun – made famous by Clint Eastwood in the film *Dirty Harry* – was only a replica.
Mirror

A naughty nurse called Janet promised kinky nights of magic to a married man who wrote her passionate love letters.

He was teased with sexy photographs, steamy suggestions and an offer to meet her at a hotel.

But soon he was being blackmailed . . . the girl of his dreams was really a man called Brian.
Mirror

As entertainment a well-told delayed-drop story is hard to beat.

Structure

News is all about answering questions – the reader's. The best guide to developing a news story is to keep asking yourself: what does the reader need or want to know now?

1 Building the pyramid

First the intro must be amplified, extended, explained, justified. For example, in a WHAT story where the main character is not named in the intro, the reader needs to know something more about them: certainly their name, probably their age and occupation, perhaps other details depending on the story. A CLAIM story where the intro gives only a general attribution – 'according to a survey' – needs a detailed attribution later on.

These are obvious, routine and in a sense formal points. Similarly, a sport story needs the score, a court story needs details of the charges, and so on.

A common development of a news intro in the classic news pyramid is to take the story it contains and then extend it:

Intro

> A six-year-old boy was rescued by firemen after he became wedged under a portable building being used as a polling station.

Extension of intro

> Jack Moore was playing with friends near his home in Nevilles Cross Road, Hebburn, South Tyneside, when curiosity got the better of him and he crawled into the eight-inch space under the building, where he became firmly wedged.
>
> Firemen used airbags to raise the cabin before Jack was freed . . .

Further information and quote

> and taken to hospital, where he was treated for cuts and bruising and allowed home. His mother, Lisa, said: 'He is a little shaken and bruised but apart from that he seems all right.'
> *Daily Telegraph*

In a longer story the intro can be extended twice, each time with more detail:

Intro

A woman artist was on the run last night after threatening to shoot three judges in the Royal Courts of Justice.

First extension of intro

Annarita Muraglia, who is in her early 20s, stood up in the public gallery brandishing what appeared to be a Luger and ran towards the judges screaming: 'If anybody moves I am going to shoot.'

Two judges tried to reason with her as the third calmly left court 7 to raise the alarm.

Within minutes armed response units and police dog handlers surrounded the huge Victorian gothic building. But Muraglia, who has twice been jailed for contempt in the past – for stripping in court and throwing paint at a judge – disappeared into the warren of corridors.

The drama brought chaos to central London for five hours as roads around the Strand were closed. As hundreds of court staff were evacuated an RAF helicopter was drafted in to help 80 police on the ground.

Second extension of intro

Witnesses said Lord Justice Beldam, 71, Mrs Justice Bracewell, 62, and Mr Justice Mance, 54, were hearing a routine criminal appeal when Muraglia – who had no connection with the case – stood up in the gallery.

'She was holding a gun American-style with both hands and seemed deranged,' said barrister Tom MacKinnon. 'She told the judges: "I demand you hear my case right now or I will start shooting."

'Mrs Justice Bracewell tried to reason with her but the woman started waving the gun, threatening to shoot anybody who moved.'

Lord Justice Beldam, one of the most senior High Court judges, calmly urged her to put down her gun as members of the public and lawyers sat in stunned silence.

Senior court registrar Roy Armstrong bravely approached her and asked for details of her case, but she then fled through a door to the judges' chambers.

Further information: background

Italy-born Muraglia, from Islington, North London, was jailed for contempt in December 1994 after breaking furniture and attacking staff at a child custody hearing.

Later, during a review of her sentence, she dropped her trousers to reveal her bare bottom painted with the words 'Happy Christmas'.

In July 1995, she sprayed green paint over the wig of Judge Andrew Brooks. The following month when he sentenced her to 15 months for contempt she again bared her bottom and was escorted away screaming: 'So you don't want to see my bottom again, Wiggy?'

Further information: update

Police said last night that they did not know if the gun was real or fake. They were confident of making an arrest.
Daily Mail

Alternatively, the intro may be followed by information on events leading up to it before the intro is restated:

Intro

Comic Eddie Izzard fought back when he was attacked in the street by an abusive drunk, a court heard yesterday.

Events leading up to intro

The award-winning comedian, who wears skirts and make-up on stage, had been taunted by jobless Matthew Dodkin after a stand-up show at the Corn Exchange, Cambridge, last November. Magistrates in the city heard that 22-year-old Dodkin had put his hands on his waist while running his tongue round his lips and saying: 'Ooh, Tracy.'

Mr Izzard admitted: 'I was very abusive towards him and I said he deserved to be cut with a knife.' . . .

Extension of intro

Dodkin then attacked him. 'I punched back and I struck blows, which is surprising because the last fight I had I was 12,' said Mr Izzard, 35, who suffered a cut lip and a black eye. . . .

Further information

Dodkin, of Queensway Flats, Cambridge, declined to give evidence after denying common assault. He was fined £120 and ordered to pay £100 compensation.
Daily Mail

The intro may be followed by explanation – of a single aspect of the intro or of the intro as a whole:

Intro

An advert for Accurist watches featuring an ultra-thin model is being investigated by the Advertising Standards Authority.

Explanation of intro

The woman has a silver watch wrapped round her upper arm, with the slogan: 'Put some weight on.'

'We're investigating it on the grounds that it might be distressing and upsetting to people with eating disorders,' said a spokesman for the authority. It had received 78 complaints from people with anorexia or bulimia, from relatives and friends of sufferers, and from the Eating Disorder Association.

Further information and quotes

An Accurist spokesman said the company had also received complaints, and claimed that the advertisement was no longer running. 'There was never any intention to cause distress,' he said. Models One, the agency used by Zoya, the model in question, said that she was naturally thin and 'an exceptionally beautiful girl'.
Guardian

Quotes from the people and organisations involved in stories are an essential part of their development. The story above, having quoted the Advertising Standards Authority, includes comments from the company and model agency. Readers – except the most bigoted – want to be given both sides of a story.

Conflicts between people and organisations – in politics, business, court cases – often make news. If the issue is complicated, the intro should be an attempt to simplify it without distortion. As the story is developed it will become easier to deal with the complications.

In the story below the reporter (or sub) has decided to lead on the technical victory won by McDonald's and not overload the intro by including the fact that two of the claims made by the Green campaigners were found to be justified. But this fact must be included early in the story.

Intro

McDonald's won a hollow victory over two Green campaigners yesterday after the longest libel trial in history.

First extension of intro

The hamburger corporation was awarded £60,000 damages over a leaflet which savaged its reputation, accusing it of putting profits before people, animal welfare and rain forests.

But the verdict cost more than £10 million in legal bills, which McDonald's will never recover from the penniless protesters who fought for three years in the High Court.

New fact

David Morris and Helen Steel were also claiming victory last night after the judge backed two of their claims. In an 800-page judgment which took six months to prepare, Mr Justice Bell ruled that the company is cruel to animals and that its advertising takes advantage of susceptible young children.

First extension of intro (continued)

Mr Morris, 43, and 31-year-old Miss Steel are refusing to pay a penny of the damages. 'They don't deserve any money,' said Miss Steel, a part-time barmaid. 'And in any case, we haven't got any.'

Further information – background

The trial began in June 1994 and spanned 314 days in court, involving 180 witnesses and 40,000 pages of documents.

At its heart was the leaflet 'What's Wrong with McDonald's?', produced by the tiny pressure group London Greenpeace, which is not connected to Greenpeace International. The defendants helped to distribute it in the 1980s.

McDonald's had issued similar libel writs many times before, and opponents had always backed down. But Mr Morris and Miss Steel, vegetarian anarchists from Tottenham, North London, were determined to fight.

The burger firm hired one of the most brilliant legal teams money can buy, headed by Richard Rampton QC. The defendants were forced to represent themselves because there is no legal aid for libel cases. Former postman Mr Morris, a single parent with an eight-year-old son, appeared in court in casual dress, usually unshaven. Miss Steel, the daughter of a retired company director from Farnham, Surrey, prepared for the case each morning while hanging from a strap on the Piccadilly Line tube.

Second extension of intro

Yesterday Mr Justice Bell ruled that they had libelled McDonald's by alleging that the corporation ripped down rain forests, contributed to Third

World starvation, created excessive waste and sold food which was closely linked with heart disease and cancer.

He said it was also libellous to claim that McDonald's was interested in recruiting only cheap labour and exploited disadvantaged groups, particularly women and black people, although the claim was 'partly justified' because the firm pays low wages.

Further information and quotes

The judge also condemned as 'most unfair' the practice of sending young staff home early if the restaurant was quiet and not paying them for the rest of their shift.

Critics of the company will also seize on his ruling that McDonald's 'are culpably responsible for cruel practices in the rearing and slaughter of some of the animals which are used to produce their food'.

After the hearing, McDonald's UK president Paul Preston said he had no wish to bankrupt Mr Morris and Miss Steel. 'This was not a matter of costs, it was a matter of truth,' he said.

But the case has been a public relations disaster for McDonald's, cast in the role of a hugely rich corporation using its financial muscle to suppress debate on important issues. Far from the leaflet being suppressed, two million copies have now been handed out around the world.

Daily Mail

2 Splitting the pyramid

The pyramid structure is far easier to sustain if the intro is single rather than double. One of the problems with A + B intros is that they are difficult to develop coherently. The double intro below illustrates the problem:

Intro (A)

Bill Clinton has completed his selection of the most diverse Cabinet in US history by appointing the country's first woman law chief.

Intro (B)

The President-elect also picked a fourth black and a second Hispanic to join his top team.

Extension of intro A

Zoe Baird, currently general counsel for the insurance company Aetna Life & Casualty, will be his Attorney General.

Extension of intro B

Black representative Mike Espy was named Mr Clinton's secretary for agriculture while former mayor of Denver Federico Pena, a Hispanic, will be responsible for transport issues.
Daily Mail

Another strategy for the double intro is to develop part A before returning to part B:

Intro (A + B)

Australian Lucas Parsons equalled the course record with a nine-under-par 64, but still could not quite take the spotlight away from Tiger Woods in the first round of the Australian Masters in Melbourne yesterday.

Extension of intro A

Parsons fired six birdies on the front nine before holing his second shot at the par four 13th for an eagle two – the highlight of the round. His approach shot landed on the green and bounced two metres beyond the flag, but then spun back into the hole.

Parsons now shares the Huntingdale course record with compatriot Mike Clayton and German Bernhard Langer.

Quotes supporting intro A

'My game has been getting better over recent months. This is a course I know and I can play well here,' said Parsons. 'I got off to a good start today and it just kept happening. I just went with the flow.'

Extension of intro B

But Woods, who won the Bangkok Classic in Thailand on Sunday, his fourth tournament victory since turning professional last August, was still the centre of attention.

Development of B and quotes

He also enjoyed the long holes to finish at five-under-par 68 for a share of fifth place to remain in contention.

The 21-year-old big-hitting American birdied all four par fives on the par-73 course to the delight of a large gallery, even though he only used his driver once.

'I grinded my way around there and came in with a good score. Off the tee, it was probably one of my better ball-striking rounds in a while,' Woods said.

'It was just the mental grind of playing a golf course that requires accuracy and so much precision off the tee. You don't really have a chance to relax.

'I haven't played my best golf today. I just made one birdie besides the par fives and that's not saying a whole lot.'

Further information

Australian Peter O'Malley held second place with a 65. Former US Masters champion Larry Mize finished on five-under alongside Woods, while defending champion Craig Parry, of Australia, struggled to a 73.
Daily Telegraph

Splitting the pyramid always presents problems. Either, as in the first example above, you make the reader hop about from A to B as the story unfolds – now it's A, now it's B. Or, as in the second example, you develop A fully before turning to B. The problem here is that B can get forgotten before the reader reaches it.

It cannot be stressed too strongly that the best intro is always the simplest: try to find one point for your intro rather than two – or more. In terms of development this may mean (as in the *Daily Mail* story on McDonald's above) that you need to introduce early in the story important material not covered by the intro. But that is a better solution than cluttering the intro and confusing the general development of the story.

3 Exceptions to the pyramid

Don't worship the pyramid: it is only a way of visualising the most common structure of a traditional news story. The guiding principle in developing a news story is: what does the reader need or want to know now? If answering their questions means abandoning the pyramid, go ahead.

Speech reports, for example, are not necessarily written in strict pyramid form. They should start with the most important point made by the speaker – but this will often be followed by other points that have little to do with the first. Of course, you should try to put these secondary points in order of importance but this may seem a pretty arbitrary process.

However, to keep the pyramid idea, each point can be seen as a mini-pyramid with its own intro, development and elaborating quote; thus the story can become a series of small pyramids.

4 The narrative style

The clearest example of non-pyramid news writing is a story in the narrative style, which begins with a dramatic moment and carries on to the end – often the point of the story. If you cut a narrative news story from the end you destroy it.

The one concession made to conventional news writing is that the main character is often asked for a quote, which is added on after the narrative ending.

Intro

When Bernard Warner examined the lobster it did not strike him as being particularly odd. The crustacean looked paler than its rivals but it had arrived at Mr Warner's fishmonger shop in Doncaster as part of a routine delivery from the East coast, so there could not be anything unusual about it, could there?

Story continues

Deciding the animal was simply suffering from old age, Mr Warner flew to Madeira on holiday. En route, his in-flight magazine fell open at an article about albino lobsters.

A white lobster caught off the American coast was sold for £15,000, the article told him. A bigger version caught off Filey was insured for £20,000.

Story ends

Mr Warner raced to a phone after touching down. 'Don't sell that lobster,' he breathlessly told his family firm. It was too late. The creature – worth £20,000 – had been sold on at the normal market rate, boiled and digested by an unsuspecting diner somewhere.

Quote

Mr Warner, who has been in the fish business for 40 years, sells his lobsters to restaurants and private customers throughout the country, and he has no idea where his prize catch went.

He said: 'I couldn't believe it. In all my time as a fishmonger I've never come across one before. I'm pig sick.'

'Someone has had a very valuable meal without even knowing it. For me it's like winning the lottery and then discovering you have thrown the ticket away.'
Guardian

News style

News style is – or ought to be – plain, simple, clear, so that the story tells itself. For a detailed discussion of this issue, see Chapter 8, 'Style', page 150.

Variation

One of the worst news-writing habits you can acquire is to avoid calling a spade a spade – or rather, having called it a spade in the intro, to insist on calling it a gardening tool, a digging device and then a horticultural implement in the pars that follow.

This practice is based on two false assumptions: one, that the repetition of words like spade is always a bad idea; two, that attentive readers enjoy these variation words for their own sake.

Precisely the opposite is true – as is shown by the story above. A lively tale about a special kind of lobster is weakened by the inept use of a series of variation words to refer to it: 'crustacean' in par one; 'animal' in par two; 'creature' in par four.

These words add nothing: they are clearly examples of variation for its own sake. And if the reader has half an ear they grate. 'Crustacean' is particularly naff: it echoes those old football reports where 'the 35-year-old goalkeeper Wally Jones' becomes 'the veteran net-minder' in the next par.

By contrast the reporter just gets away with 'prize catch' in par five – though it would have been better if Mr Warner had done the catching in the first place. But it was a prize; it had been caught; and the phrase adds the right kind of emphasis.

Some ten years after the lobster story quoted above the *Guardian* published a news feature about the increasing popularity of the shellfish best known as 'langoustines' (that's the French word – they're also known by their Italian name 'scampi' and as Dublin Bay prawns and Norway lobsters). According to the gourmet's bible, *Larousse Gastronomique*, 'This marine crustacean of the lobster family resembles a freshwater crayfish' – not, you'll notice, a prawn. But in the *Guardian* piece the words 'langoustine' and 'prawn' are used interchangeably. The picture caption, for example, reads:

> Frank Ronald . . . sorts a day's catch of langoustine after returning to Loch Fyne, Argyll. The prawn is about to hit the mass market . . .

This kind of variation has traditionally been called 'elegant' – because it's intended to embellish, to add colour to copy. But it rarely adds anything – except confusion.

Then there is variation to avoid unintended repetition. Your ear should tell you when this is necessary. But remember that the plainer the word the less noticeable it is when repeated, so don't bother to avoid repeating words like 'said' and 'says'.

Sometimes repetition tells you that the sentence itself is badly constructed – too long, too loose, too complicated. Here's an example with the repeated word in italic type:

> A mother of three young *children*, jailed for two months after lying about a traffic accident, was yesterday reunited with her *children* after she was freed by three Appeal Court judges – but they reiterated the gravity of the offence and said the plight of her *children* had tipped the balance in favour of her release.
> Guardian

About the only thing to be said in favour of this intro is that 'children' does not become 'offspring' in the second case and 'progeny' or 'issue' in the third. If you find yourself writing a sentence like this, don't struggle to replace the repeated words: rewrite the sentence altogether in a simpler way.

Quotes

First, in general, use 'said'/'says' to introduce and attribute quotes, though 'told'/'tells' is a useful variation, as in 'the minister told MPs'. So do not write:

> Speaking at the meeting the speaker said . . .

but:

> The speaker told the meeting . . .

Always avoid variations like 'claim', 'admit', 'state', 'remark', 'point out', 'explain', 'refute' – unless you intend the precise meaning conveyed by the word.

Do not use 'he added' because you think the quote has been going on long enough and are too lazy to think up some other way of getting to the next bit. Keep 'he added' for cases where there is a pause, an afterthought or a contrast as in:

> He said it would probably rain – but he added: 'We need it.'

Where possible use the present tense – 'says' – instead of the past – 'said'. When somebody is quoted for the first time put the attribution at the beginning, as in:

> John Smith says: 'I'm furious.'

If the attribution does not come at the beginning, put it after the first complete sentence – not in the middle of it and not at the end of the complete quote. This is the way to do it:

> 'I'm furious,' John Smith says. 'I've never been so angry.'

Consistency

Be consistent. Don't change your tone in the middle of a story. Either write in the traditional style or use one of the variations; be serious or light – not both at the same time.

Particularly avoid the facetious remark dropped into a straightforward story. As the columnist Keith Waterhouse once put it:

> The interpolation of a weak joke into a serious news story is so inappropriate that it can only be described as oafish.

Bridges and links

In general news does not need bridges to connect one par with the next. Transitional words and phrases like 'also' – or the pompous equivalent 'in addition' – are rarely necessary. When you start a new sentence or a new par you are effectively saying to the reader: 'also'. That does not mean that these words and phrases are always wrong but you should not strain to include them in traditional news stories.

Journalese and jargon

Most of what is called journalese – whether downmarket ('axe' for 'sack') or upmarket ('sustain injury' for 'be hurt') – is bad writing and you should avoid it. 'Following' for 'after' is certainly an example of this.

But certain code words can be useful – to maximise the amount of information you can convey to the reader. For example, if you're pretty confident – but not certain – that A will happen, you can write: 'A is set to happen.' You should always try to find out precisely what somebody's role is in something – but if you can't, it's usually better to write 'B is involved with the project' rather than nothing at all.

The same advice covers phrases like 'industry sources say' when your contacts will not give you identified quotes. Inform your reader – but keep the jargon under control.

Names and titles

The convention in journalism is full name ('John/Joan Smith') for the first use, then either courtesy title ('Mr/Mrs/Miss/Ms Smith') or surname or first name for the rest of the story. (For more on this and similar points see *Subediting and Production for Journalists*.) Remember, be consistent: never follow 'John Smith' by 'Mr Smith', then 'John'. Again, variation for its own sake irritates the reader.

Endings

In general, traditional news stories (as opposed to those in the narrative style) do not have endings – that is, they end where the writer runs out of steam, the sub runs out of space, the reader runs out of interest. But there is no reason why a news story should not end neatly. The exception proves that the rule is one of pragmatism not principle:

> BT is tightening up its telephone security system after its confidential list of ex-directory numbers was penetrated – by a woman from Ruislip.
>
> Working from home, Rachel Barry, a middle-aged married mother, conned BT into revealing the ex-directory numbers of celebrities, sports stars and people in the news . . .
>
> Last week Mrs Barry was convicted by Harrow magistrates of 12 offences of obtaining personal data and selling it to national newspapers . . .
>
> It is believed Mrs Barry had been operating the scam for several years and had earned thousands of pounds. She pleaded guilty to all 12 offences and was fined a total of £1,200 and ordered to pay costs of £800.
>
> Last night the *Observer* was unable to contact Mrs Barry by telephone. She is ex-directory.
> *Observer*

That is an ending.

Two news stories

MAN KILLED AS L-DRIVE CAR PLUNGES OFF CLIFF

A man was feared dead last night after his car ran off a 150ft clifftop into rough seas when his girlfriend lost control while he was giving her a driving lesson.

The woman, in her early 20s, scrambled from the Ford Fiesta as it crashed through a low stone wall at the edge of a car park at the Beacon, St Agnes, on the north Cornwall coast.

Andrew Dunklin, 25, from St Agnes, was trapped in the vehicle as it rolled over the cliff. It is thought he was thrown through the windscreen into the sea. The car came to rest in 30ft of water and immediately began to break up.

The woman raised the alarm and coastguards launched a rescue operation which at its height involved a Navy helicopter, divers, two lifeboats and a cliff rescue team.

Insp Paul Whetter of Devon & Cornwall police said the woman had managed to get out just before the car went over the cliff.

She was treated for shock at the scene by paramedics before being taken to Treliske Hospital in Truro.

A neighbour looking after the missing man's mother at her home in the village said: 'She has just lost her only son.'

The search operation was hampered by worsening weather and a Navy diver had to be pulled out of the sea. The St Agnes and St Ives inshore lifeboats could not get close to the spot.

'We sent our cliff man down to a point about 60ft above the waves, where the cliff became a sheer drop,' said Mike North, sector manager with HM Coastguard. 'He was able to keep an eye on the scene and spotted a lot of debris from the car.

'He saw some clothing and the inshore lifeboat was able to pick up the girl's bag floating in the water.'

A spokesman for RNAS Culdrose added: 'The first diver in the water said it was too dangerous for others to go in. He was being pounded by pieces of wreckage from the car which was being smashed on to the rocks at the bottom of the cliffs.'

The search was called off at 5pm because the situation had become 'too dangerous' for rescue workers. It was to be resumed at first light today.

Mr Dunklin is understood to have been giving his girlfriend a driving lesson on Beacon Road, a remote and little-used track near the cliffs. They may have driven into the gravel-surfaced car park to practise reversing or three-point turns.
Daily Telegraph

This is a stark and terrible story simply told. The reporter has no need to strain for effect here.

The intro is a bit long at 31 words – a tabloid would have shortened 'when his girlfriend lost control while he was giving her a driving lesson' to something like 'when a driving lesson went wrong'. But because the words and clauses are straightforward, the intro works well enough.

Then, because the intro tells so much of the story, the second par can add dramatic detail as well as locating the story. But do we really want to know what make of car it was? Well, yes, the ordinariness of the Ford Fiesta helps to make this a story about any young couple.

The third par retells the intro; the fourth introduces the rescue operation; but rather than turn the story sideways to cover the search, the reporter rightly concentrates on the two people involved in the accident – and the man's mother.

When we get to it, halfway through the story, the search is described with the aid of powerful quotes. Finally, there's a par on how the couple came to be at the clifftop.

A few quibbles: 'vehicle' in the third par is unnecessary variation for 'car': it follows 'Ford Fiesta'; RNAS (towards the end) should be given in full; in the same par 'added' is particularly strange, suggesting that the two people quoted were in the same room – and the woman would surely be named if police had released her name.

But in general the reporter has made good use of an opportunity to let a strong story tell itself without clutter and melodramatic language.

HOBBIES PUT JUDGE ON THE ROAD TO RUIN

A judge's entry in *Who's Who* listed his passions as cars and drinking with friends. Yesterday these twin interests landed John Aspinall QC in court, where he was banned from the road for two and a half years for drink-driving.

Aspinall, 50, who worked as a lorry driver before becoming a lawyer, was more than three times over the limit when he caused a crash on Good Friday.

In *Who's Who* he lists his recreations as 'motor sports' and 'being with my wife and friends at the Drax Arms' – the country pub near his home in Spetisbury, Dorset, where he is a popular regular.

Now his career is in tatters. He has resigned as a crown court recorder, a part-time judge, and faces a Bar Council disciplinary hearing which could mean being suspended from practising as a barrister or even thrown out of the profession.

He has also resigned from the judicial committee of the governing body of the RAC motorsports council.

Magistrates at Blandford in Dorset were told Aspinall had a blood alcohol level of 122mg. The legal limit is 35mg. He admitted drink-driving and was fined £1,800 and told his ban could be cut by six months if he takes a driver-rehabilitation course.
Daily Mail

A routine 'judge banned for drink-driving' court report has been turned into a lively story because somebody has bothered to check Aspinall's entry in *Who's Who*.

The all-important intro is a form of delayed drop: the first sentence sets up the second. Then after some basic information on the offence, the sequence is repeated: quotes from *Who's Who* are followed by more on Aspinall's ruined career.

Only in the last par do we get the details of the offence and the magistrates' decision. This must appear somewhere in the story – but only as a tailpiece.

There are blemishes: 'twin interests' in the second sentence is a curious variation on 'passions' in the first; and there is a clumsy phrase in the fourth par, 'which could mean being suspended'.

But, as a whole, the story is a good example of news writing, which grabs the reader's attention, then keeps it by answering their questions.

3
Writing features

Sally Adams

The joy of feature writing lies in its variety. Anything from a celebrity interview to an agony column, a product round-up to an obit, can be called a feature. But because they are so varied features are hard to define. The safest guide is negative: they're not news.

Not being news, they're liberated from spare, functional prose. In place of the breathless messenger they can be entertaining gossips, perceptive analysts, eccentric experts, sympathetic counsellors, bitchy snoops, inspiring guides.

Because they're so varied they're harder to write. They build on what's learnt as a news reporter and also demand that writers attract and hold the reader's attention without the advantage of a simple pattern to follow. And they often require that writers research and master complicated subjects, then reduce huge chunks of information to accessible, digestible copy.

Whereas reporters work with formulas, feature writers generally don't. Ask five journalists to cover a car crash and they'll deliver recognisably similar copy. Ask the same five to write a feature on car crashes and, first, you'll be asked what publication it's for; then you're likely to receive five very different features, each aimed at a selected audience. Feature writing requires a different way of thinking, writing and structuring.

Now, more than ever, a feature writer is likely to be a freelance rather than a staff journalist. Most of what follows applies particularly to the writer who may be approaching a publication for the first time.

Guidelines

Though feature writers are not burdened by lengthy rules, there are some guidelines and a few imperatives. The most important are:

- Know who you're writing for, their interests and concerns. Otherwise how can you gain and retain their attention?
- Know what you want to say and achieve. Take time to write a brief: it pays rich dividends.
- Think, think, think – and go on thinking. Feature writers are valued for the freshness of their approach.

Effective feature writing is accessible, interesting, lively, colourful, grabbing and relevant. For writers to achieve these results depends, first, on accepting a simple principle: the communicator takes total responsibility for getting the message across.

In ascending order of difficulty, features can inform, help, amuse, persuade and inspire to action. Gradations exist within all these categories. The difficulty in writing to 'inform', for example, ranges from providing coherent and accessible data to offering analysis and promoting understanding. 'Persuade' ranges in difficulty from prompting a reader to try a new hairstyle to convincing them they should adopt a new lifestyle.

A study of what editors and features editors look for produced remarkably similar answers. Features should:

- involve the reader
- be accurate
- be readable
- have a grabbing intro
- meet the brief
- have substance
- be well crafted
- contain ... (the X factor: an added element of surprise on a subject specific to the publication).

Types of feature

Most features fall into one of four main categories:

1 Profiles
  (a) of individuals, usually based on interviews plus press cuttings, which can be either written in the first person ('A life in the day', *Sunday Times* Magazine), ghosted or reported in the third person; or edited, eg from a tape, into the Q&A format; or emailed in reply to set questions (questionnaire). If the subject is dead the profile becomes an obit, written by acquaintance, friend, admirer or enemy – or compiled in-house from cuttings.

(b) of two or more people or groups or organisations, again based on interviews plus cuttings. Subjects can be companies, rock groups, sports teams, clubs, councils . . .

2   News and issues-related features, eg backgrounders, which put news in context; retrospectives, which look back at past stories; and features based on current issues or special investigations. A 'news feature' is a hybrid, somewhere between a straightforward news story and a conventional feature. Colour pieces describe events as they happen and are particularly used for funerals and sporting events.

3   Product stories about a single product/round-up of many, described, compared, tested.

4   Opinion and comment, eg leaders/editorials, think pieces, columns, diaries.

Rating impact

When editors and features editors receive fresh copy they don't tick boxes as they read. But they are looking for the answers to certain vital questions. As a former chairman of the Man Booker Prize panel put it, when confronted by a new novel:

> Personally, I found myself asking four questions. . . . Could I read it? If I could read it, did I believe it? If I believed it, did I care about it? If I cared, what was the quality of my caring, and would it last?

> Few, very few, survived as far as question four. Far too many relied on the classic formula of a beginning, a muddle and an end.
> Philip Larkin

Applying these questions to a feature means asking:

1   Did I read it to the end? Was it smoothly written, taking me effortlessly from A to Z?

2   If I read to the end, was I convinced by what I read? Was it accurate and authoritative?

3   If I was convinced, did I care? Was it relevant? Did I feel involved?

4   Now, if I cared, am I going to do anything about it? Cut out and keep the feature? Show it to friends? Write to the editor? Follow the expert advice? Learn from that example? Put those suggestions into practice?

A quick word before you start

The quality of the questions you ask yourself before you start writing is crucial. The sharper your questions, the more likely you are to produce good copy.

As always, writing for your readers is the key. This doesn't mean playing safe and giving them more of what they liked last time. Slavishly following market research has been the death of many a publication. Offer readers an amalgam of known success with a dash of surprise. 'I want to see five new facts in every feature,' demanded the first, highly successful editor of *Marie Claire*.

Before even thinking about feature ideas, wise writers make certain that they know the publication's editorial policy. Common examples include: to inform, to help, to improve, to unite, to enthuse, to persuade, to entertain, to inspire. Clearly, the words chosen 'to inform' will be different from those chosen 'to persuade', requiring differing approaches and vocabulary.

Now for the readers – getting to know them is essential:

- circulation (how many buy/subscribe to the publication or receive free copies)
- readership (how many read the publication)
- average age range
- male/female split
- years of education – this affects words used and sentence complexity
- interests
- job title for b2b
- disposable income of consumer publications (general public) or budget available (b2b)
- where readers live
- political/religious/social views
- what makes them happy
- their greatest anxieties
- if known, how long they spend reading the publication.

The same . . . but different

Whatever type of publication a journalist writes for – newspaper, consumer magazine, b2b magazine, newsletter – the basic approach is the same: write for your readers.

Journalists writing for newspapers and consumer magazines usually know more about their subjects than most of their readers, so their main task is to capture their interest. However, with b2b magazines the readers themselves are specialists who often know more about the business than the writer does. This presents the journalist with different challenges but also rewards. With the thousands of b2b magazines published in the UK there is obviously a market for feature writers prepared to specialise.

Feature process

Once the foundations are laid, the feature process can begin. For complex articles it runs this way: *idea, brief, research, interview, plan, write*. For simpler, say first-person, features it's possible to go straight from *brief* to *plan*, as the writer has lived the research and has no need to self-interview.

Features start from an *idea*, which should suit the publication and interest the readership. There are few, if any, that are completely new. Two initial factors to consider are time and manageability. It's best to avoid features needing quotes from European academics in August, for example, because of the summer holidays. Similarly, avoid features that need phone interviews with Singapore business executives for a UK publication because of the time difference, unless you are able to work very early in the morning or late at night.

Ideas like 'music in the movies' or 'miscarriages of justice' aren't features, they're books. It's essential to slice them into manageable proportions, looking at trends in three recent British movie scores, for example, or examining four current justice campaigns. The more frequent the publication, the thinner the slice. Salami for dailies, thick toast for monthlies.

The *brief* is where many beginners go wrong, mostly because they consider it a waste of time. Far from it: a well-thought-out brief provides direction and shape. Ideally it should include:

- deadline
- length
- the angle/approach you are adopting
- the tone (campaigning/informative/entertaining . . .)
- the scope/limits of the feature – what you plan to include/omit
- what's wanted: colourful quotes; background information; detailed facts; analysis . . .
- questions you want answered
- questions the editor wants answered
- where to go for research
- any extras: boxes, stat tables, pictures, illustrations.

Beware the editor/features editor who refuses to brief, saying airily 'You know what I want'. Experience shows this often involves a complex subject not thought through carefully enough. Editors may have a fuzzy notion of what they think they want but they know exactly what they *don't* want when they see it. If you are not given a brief, you should work one out, then go back and agree it with your editor.

A brief provides the basic structure and eases you into the next stage: *research*. But be warned: there's a lot of inaccurate info on the web. Use but don't rely on Google. If you are interested in what appears to be a relevant report, quote or interview, then check the original source and *date* very carefully. The info could be years old and could land you and the publication in serious difficulty. Corroborate any stats that could be dodgy, double-check when possible and never trust spelling on the web, even on home pages.

Original research and interviews often provide the bonus that editors prize: fresh facts, lively and unexpected quotes, copy that elicits the 'never-knew-that' reaction. Don't rush here. Start early, think laterally, go to a reliable source and note sources. Stick with research. Make that extra phone call. Dig for that extra hour.

The *interview*[1] stage comes next. Think, analyse, plan and focus as before. Don't start until you know what you want to know. If you're interviewing someone experienced at dealing with journalists, try to make it interesting for them too – and remember they're used to journalistic wiles. Never ask celebrities the first question that springs to mind: it's likely to have sprung to every other mind as well. Celebrities apart, always ask the obvious as well as stimulating questions. With most feature subjects, the skill is to get them to drop their defences and talk.

Go in/pick up the phone only when you are thoroughly prepared and know exactly what you want to know. Don't talk too much but listen intently and intelligently to what's said and, finally, swap places and consider the impact of your questions. You won't get a good interview with a research scientist who uses vivisection if you start 'How can you possibly be involved in such a contemptible business?'

Be sceptical not adversarial. Hostile questions elicit good quotes but it's best to start nice and turn nasty later. Remember that 'you get more flies with honey than vinegar'. And never, ever, forget that they are the star, and are not there simply to provide you with required facts or opinions.

Once you've completed the research and interviewing, pause. It's too soon to start writing. *Plan* your structure. You don't have to follow it slavishly, but forethought pays dividends in saving time and preventing angst.

Structure

Of all the stages in feature writing planning structure is the most difficult. The brief may be the most neglected, but its requirements are clear and, once

---

1 See *Interviewing for Journalists*.

followed, provide a workable guide to what is wanted. The material gathered may differ from what was planned but the task of structuring remains the same: to select what's relevant and integrate the material into a smooth-running whole.

This is not easy and short-cut solutions have been devised which bypass the need to learn to structure features copy: putting it into chart form or a prede-termined layout, four case histories, an intro and a box, for example. Speedy, straightforward – but no help when it comes to writing longer and/or more complicated features.

Trainee journalists naturally look for a formula to follow and many become uneasy when they can't find one. They have to accept that features are custom-made. Editors whose writers use a single template soon spot it and sigh 'Here we go again, starting with a quote . . .' or 'Not another "There I woz with. . ."'.

Clearly, the approach to adopt is the one that is right for that feature for that publication.

Where to begin?

First go back to your brief. If you discover gaps, plug them. Then read and reread your research and interview notes until you have assimilated them. During this process information on various aspects of the feature should be drawn together.

Take a subject like successful fund-raising with the angle 'making it profit-able and fun'. Interviews with several practised fund-raisers might yield information on events that aim to provide maximum income from minimum effort, advice on motivating helpers, tips on planning enjoyable campaigns, suggestions on recruiting committee members, crazy ideas that children like, warnings about legal requirements and details of helpful books.

These become headings under which each fund-raiser's thoughts are collated. One way to organise your material is to use a variant of the mind map idea first popularised by Tony Buzan in the 1970s. Take a large sheet of blank paper and in the middle put a sketch or diagram of the subject to help focus the mind; then scatter your headings randomly. Ring them, leaving plenty of space, and from your notes add the best quotes, facts, anecdotes – whatever – under each one.

When you've done this, decide what you want to say. Answer the key question – how you phrase it doesn't matter; it can be any variation on:

What's the storyline?

What's the point I want to make?

What do I want the reader to take away from this feature?

If in doubt, rehearse to yourself the subject, publication and readers. For example: 'I'm writing a feature on – for the publication – whose readers are – and what I want them to take away is –.'

Don't start writing yet

When you know what you want to say, work out a running order that will carry the reader with you from A to Z. Look at your source material, now collected under various headings. And as with news the intro is all-important: what's the best way of ensuring that the reader starts reading? What's

- the most startling fact you've discovered?
- the best anecdote?
- the most revealing quote?
- the most surprising event?

And when you've decided where to start, where next? One way is to look at the ringed headings and plot the feature's progress with arrows and links. It's important to keep information on topics together and not jump around all over the place.

After being told this one American journalist said: 'My first reaction was "obviously"; my second "but why didn't it ever occur to me?"; and my third that this was one of those banalities that "everyone knows – after they've been told".'

Some writers number each piece of research and then go for the Chinese takeaway approach: 'I'll start with 19, follow it with 15, then 22, 13, 4 . . .' Others go from reading their notes to making a simple list. This is difficult so be careful.

Well-crafted, a feature can be a must-follow yellow-brick road. But badly done it becomes a confusing maze of dead ends without even a street sign to help the reader escape. They will follow meandering footpaths or four-lane motorways if the route looks interesting and is well marked. They stop reading if confused.

Clive James's first job on the *Sydney Morning Herald* was rewriting 'casuals' (amateur contributions). He said later: 'Those months doing rewrites were probably the best practical training I ever received. Gradually the sheer weight of negative evidence began to convince me that writing is essentially a matter of saying things in the right order.'

(See also 'More on structure', page 73)

NEED-TO-DECIDE FACTORS

Publication? Are you writing for what used to be called a broadsheet, tabloid or redtop newspaper, a consumer magazine, customer magazine, business magazine, technical, trade or specialist magazine or newsletter?

Readers? Do you know the publication's editorial policy? Do you know as much as possible about the readers?

Content and approach? How many words are wanted? There is a vast choice from 8,000 (*Vanity Fair*), down to 'featurettes' at 300–350. Some writers aim to deliver *slightly* more than required as it's easier to cut than fill.

Deadline? Try to be realistic.

Genre/type? Will the feature be news-pegged (inspired by or linked to a news story), investigative, a think piece (your views on a given subject), analysis (subject assessed with pro and con quotes and facts), a personalised column?

Subject/angle? Huge choice again: celebrities are astonishingly popular as subjects, with angles being almost anything – celebrity profile, celebrity gossip, fashion, heartbreak, new house, new dog – there seems no end; business ditto; individuals or groups (sports teams, orchestras, clubs, councils); specialist topics (fashion, cooking, motoring, travel, history, jobs, children); product stories/reviews/tests?

Approach/tone? Will the feature be informative, helpful, inspiring, campaigning, funny, critical?

Style? What's wanted? Lots of quotes, anecdotes, facts, info from cuttings, research, 'colour' (copy focusing on description or impression, subjective approach)?

Display/appearance? Solid text or separated sections, case histories?

Extras? Stats, tables, boxes, pull quotes, summaries?

Intros

As was said earlier, the intro is all-important – and can take a lot of time to get right. The examples that follow can't please everyone; that's a given. But if your first reaction is to dismiss any of them out of hand, you should ask yourself whether you are responding as yourself rather than as a reader of the particular publication.

> It's no good standing there at the beginning of an article flexing your muscles. Just do the old handspring right away.
> 'Cassandra', *Mirror*

The subs and the editor are paid to read what you write; readers you have to grab. Most glance first at the headline, illustrations, maybe the standfirst (short informative display copy giving an idea of the feature's content). Only then do they read the intro. You have ten seconds max in which to catch them.

> *Sesame Street* lied. America's not full of black and white kids, all learning together in multi-racial harmony. Down in LA, Big Bird's toting an AK and the Cookie Monster's doing crack.
> *Big Issue*

The power of this intro lies in its opening sentence, with the strong and unexpected verb 'lied'. '*Sesame Street* has been lying' wouldn't work as well.

The powerful start is followed with rich examples that conjure up funny, dramatic pictures. The rhythm of the last sentence works because it's in the right order, nailed down at the end by the single syllable 'crack'. It would be less effective if the Cookie Monster preceded Big Bird. If you doubt this, read the transposed sentence aloud.

> The groom fell asleep in his mother's lap. The bride burst into tears and had to be silenced with a piece of fruit. Dhanraj was four, his bride Santosh was seven. The wedding, which would change their lives for ever, meant nothing to them. It was their parents who recited the marriage vows, their parents who circled the sacred fire seven times on their small and sleepy children's behalf.
> Rosalyn Chissick, *Elle*

Here's another example of surprising juxtaposition: childhood and marriage. All the words are carefully chosen. 'Recited' has greater ceremonial overtones than 'repeated'. 'Silenced' rather than 'comforted' shows that something important is happening. The 'sacred fire' and 'seven' import mystic hints about a solemn ceremony, contrasting with the touching 'small and sleepy children'.

There's no one way to write an intro, only the way that's right for the feature and the publication. The approach you select should spring from what you judge will most interest your readers. Content and style both have their part to play. The test of a good intro is whether it grabs and keeps the reader's attention, making them want to read on.

Intros to avoid are those which bemuse, bore and activate the switch-off factor. So swap heads with the readers and avoid anything they could consider trite, banal, convoluted, negative, patronising or irrelevant and don't include too many sets of initials, abbreviations or acronyms. Worst of all, don't write anything that can be dismissed with a weary 'So what?'

Types of intro

These five categories are useful as guides; in practice, many excellent intros combine two or more elements.

Strong/provocative/intriguing statement
Narrative/anecdote
Description/scene-setting
Question that buttonholes the reader
Quote

1 Statement

The most common way to start a feature, capable of almost infinite variation. Usually relies for impact on contrast, colour and surprise.

> We British still lead the world in something. Unfortunately, it's tabloid journalism.
> Adam Sweeting, *Guardian*

A straightforward, hard-to-resist first sentence. Opinionated second sentence, spot-on for *Guardian* readers. It's a variation of the 'build' em up, knock 'em down' approach, with the punch words at the end.

> Sir Alex Ferguson's secret dressing-room doctrine – cornerstone of his sustained success at Manchester United – can finally be revealed to the outside world.
> David McDonnell, *Mirror*

Irresistible – even to those who don't play football, don't follow football, don't care about football. To prove the point, here's the dressing-room doctrine (if you don't read on, you're a very rare person indeed):

> The SIX most important words: 'I ADMIT I MADE A MISTAKE'.
> The FIVE most important words: 'YOU DID A GOOD JOB'.
> The FOUR most important words: 'WHAT IS YOUR OPINION?'
> The THREE most important words: 'IF YOU PLEASE'.
> The TWO most important words: 'THANK YOU'.
> The ONE most important word: 'WE'.
> The LEAST important word: 'I'.

Now you know. It's understandably preachy and just a tad disappointing that it's so simple – but the intro works.

Lauren Bacall is not a legend. Not yet, anyway. 'If I'm a legend, I'm dead,' she says. 'Do you want me to be dead? Legends are of the past.' This is typical Bacall: 82 years old she may be, but she remains as bold, bullish and brassy as the day she first sauntered onto the screen more than 60 years ago. The woman once dubbed The Look now just shoots them with those steely grey eyes of hers. 'I have no respect for celebrities,' she continues, 'and I object to being called one, so don't try it! I'm an actress, not a celebrity.'
James Mottram, *Independent*

The short, sharp, surprising first sentence is suddenly put into perspective by an even shorter, sharper second sentence. The next two are just as condensed. All define the Bacall territory. In just 29 words Bacall's character has been vividly established.

Words quick-march on. Her age is revealed, then her personality captured in three cunningly chosen adjectives which have a rhythm approaching a chant: bold, bullish and brassy . . . bold, bullish and brassy. So the par continues, slowing down with 'sauntered', then speeding up again for the summary, another broadside from Bacall making it clear exactly how she wants to be treated. 'I'm an actress, not a celebrity.' By quoting this, Mottram in effect says: 'This is Lauren Bacall. I'm going to play by her rules because I know this way she'll talk.' Which she did.

I hate kids. Hate them all without exception. Even yours. Especially yours. Especially if it's a boy and you named it Jake. And if you've ever written a chummy diary article about Jake for a Sunday supplement, I wish nothing short of death upon you. Death by wasps and bombs and razorwire. In a thunderstorm. While Jake looks on in horror. Because I hate parents too.
Charlie Brooker, *Guardian*

A machinegun-like attack, provocative by design, super-opinionated, meant to infuriate and entertain. He only does it to annoy because he knows . . . well, he knows it will prompt lots of emails, letters and phone calls to the editor, which is one certain way of upping your value (see 'Rating impact', page 43). Brooker makes a living from scoffing, attacking, belittling, questioning but also (occasionally) from saluting, praising and approving, all in ways that involve readers. Not easy.

A statue in his honour, a guest slot in *The Simpsons* and more appearances in the *Daily Mirror* than David Beckham. Not bad for a man who's never done a stroke of work in his life. It's Mr Andy Capp.
Jeremy Armstrong, *Mirror*

At first – no doubt – it's about a person. Who could that be? Someone who rated a statue . . . who featured in a world-famous TV cartoon . . . who has never worked . . .? Then comes the 'Gotcha!' It's Andy Capp, the cartoon character. The writer skilfully catches the readers out in very much the same way that Andy Capp always escapes work (the feature was to celebrate his fiftieth birthday).

Fashion gets more pages than ever now, with descriptive captions giving way to sharp, stylish writing.

> Finally, after several seasons lurking about at the edge of the party like a shy guest in the wrong dress, the 80s trend has taken off. Just when you thought it was safe to ditch the leggings, a herd of other dinosaur outfits from 20 years ago is congregating on the horizon, about to stampede. Prepare yourself for a renaissance of extended shoulders, outsized knitwear, masses of black, acres of cling and – crucially – the funny little pixie boot.
> Mimi Spencer, YOU

Sometimes one judiciously selected word is a sufficient hook.

> This week's deplorable idea comes from [name]
> Times diary

It's very hard not to read on to find out what the *Times* business diarist so reviled.

2 Narrative/anecdote

> The scene was Kitzbuhel, the programme *Grandstand*. The event was the men's downhill. A man referred to as 'Britain's sole representative' came plummeting down the Streif. 'He won't be looking for a first place today,' said David Vine, 'he'll be looking for experience.'

> At that very instant – not a bit later, but while David was actually saying it – Britain's sole representative was upside down and plummeting into the crowd at 60mph plus. Spectators were mown down as if by grape-shot. The air was full of snow, beanies, mittens, bits of wood. You had to be watching to get the full impact. It was a kind of perfection.
> Clive James, *Observer*

The first two matter-of-fact sentences set the scene and get the intro swinging along freely. The first hint of something out of the ordinary comes with 'A man referred to', which is taken up and echoed to great effect in the second paragraph.

Consider, too, the use of the word 'plummeting'. Is there any other word that would do as well? 'Plummet' comes from the French *plomb* meaning lead, and it gives the feeling of a headlong descent as the skier descends almost vertically. There's no other word that works as well. The well-placed quote follows, broken up with the attribution to the hapless David Vine so that the full weight of the sentence falls on the key word 'experience'.

The second paragraph begins plainly but after the first phrase, 'At that very instant', goes into 'freeze frame' or slow motion as the writer repeats what he said earlier but at greater length. This works because it mirrors what people involved in traffic accidents experience, using a device beloved of film-makers: that slowing down at moments of intensity.

Earlier the skier was allowed just the one action word 'plummeting'. Now he's shown pictorially at greater length and the rest of the description works so well because it uses specific words: snow, beanies (bobble ski hats), mittens, bits of wood. All chosen to give the feeling of fragmentation and chaos.

> It was when Michael Howard shifted into the conditional mood that I knew which side of the Atlantic I was really on. 'On Friday,' he said, 'Britain could wake up to a brighter future.' COULD? You mean ... it might not happen? If this had been Detroit or San Diego or Dubuque, incredulous staffers would have rushed the candidate off podium for emergency reprogramming. 'WILL, Michael,' they would chant patiently at him until he Got It. 'Never so much as breathe a possibility of defeat.'
> Simon Schama, *Guardian*

Schama is describing an election speech by a British politician. He deftly appeals to both the learned (the conditional? Of course, we remember our English/French/Latin grammar lessons) and the curious (what's that then?) and quickly shows everybody what he's on about. 'COULD' in caps is unmistakable.

> Exactly one year ago today, I tried to kill myself. Fortunately (or unfortunately as I felt at the time), I am blessed with an iron constitution. At 3.20am, I woke up. Through some sick irony (who says the heavens don't have a sense of humour?), it was the same time, to the minute, that I had been waking for a year before I was finally diagnosed with clinical depression.
> Sally Brampton, *Daily Telegraph*

Dramatic but not dramatised start, followed straight away by revealing details. The use of brackets is frowned on by many writers but is acceptable here exactly because they emphasise that her thought relates to the past. Then comes the strange coincidence of waking at the same time, another wry aside, and the par ends with the reason for the whole story. Straightforward writing, powerful and honest.

Journalist-describes-meeting-famous-interviewee is one of the most common ways to begin a celebrity feature. So common, in fact, that it can be deadly boring, a real heart-sinker. It's partly a reaction to the power of PRs who can determine times, limits and subjects that can be covered. So make the interview lively for the reader and as interesting as you can for the interviewee. The more famous the celebrity, the harder it is for the interviewer. One approach: go for revealing observations.

> Jack Dee is assiduously polite to the girl who serves him a cappuccino at his London club. He smiles, moves aside any clutter from the table and

says 'thank-you' twice. When she leaves he comments on how good the service is. It is something he always notices. He has never forgotten his days as a waiter.
Daily Express Saturday magazine

3 Description/scene-setting

A big-boned young man with wild hair escaping in all directions from under his baseball cap crouches by a jungle river, so excited that he can barely breathe. 'This is it! This is the one . . . a species completely new to horticulture in Britain,' he gasps. For a few magnificent moments, at this key point in his quest to track down extraordinary plants in the Australian rainforest, Tom Hart Dyke looks like Indiana Jones finding the Holy Grail – provided, that is, you ignore the giant yellow-and-white daisy printed on his sweaty T-shirt.
Sandy Mitchell, *Daily Telegraph*

Very visual. The first sentence evokes a colourful picture of a passionate gardener at his moment of triumph and it does so in the present tense, using only adjectives to draw the picture. The remaining description comes from selected nouns and active verbs. His hair is escaping, he crouches, he can barely breathe. The quote in the second sentence captures his excitement, followed by a very necessary explanation of why he is there, reinforcing the find with a touch of showbiz.

Marco Pierre White, fat hands waving, pale brown eyes staring . . . has been awake all night, 20 hours in a solicitor's office discussing a 'huge deal' and you can smell his armpits a table away.
Katharine Viner, *Guardian*

Sometimes a few colourful adjectives are necessary. Nice catering touch, 'a table away'.

Here's a feature about a detox programme run by Buddhist monks in Thailand:

It's a tidal wave of puke. Like a line of wells simultaneously striking oil, fountains of sick erupt from the mouths of the four drug addicts. The clear fluid arcs four feet through the air and splatters the earth before the kneeling junkies.
Maxim

Targeted at *Maxim*'s body-function-obsessed readers. Visual rather than smell-oriented, thank goodness. Lots of movement words: sick 'erupts', fluid 'arcs' and 'splatters'. Keeps to the vernacular with 'puke' and 'sick' rather than 'vomit'.

When the kid in the front row at the rally bit off the tip of his little finger and wrote KIM DAE JUNG in blood on his fancy white ski jacket – I think that was the first time I ever really felt like a foreign correspondent. I mean, here was something really fucking *foreign*.
P J O'Rourke, *Rolling Stone*

Straight in at the deep end with a bizarre incident. Take the 'fancy white' out of the description of the jacket and the intro doesn't work so well – the blood loses its colour. Unerringly sets the scene for a violent review of South Korean elections, which ends with O'Rourke getting tear-gassed.

4 Question that buttonholes the reader

Designed to intrigue and make the reader think. The question needs to be right for the readers, or it runs the risk of a 'couldn't care less' response.

> In the name of faith, hope and especially charity, will the people of Great Britain please put their clothes back on? This instant. Right now. Without delay. What we mean is, what has got into you all?
> Jan Moir, *Daily Telegraph*

A pleading, grossly overstated appeal in the form of a question, laden with religious overtones and addressed to the entire nation, begins a feature about the nude calendar craze started by a Women's Institute in Yorkshire. For impact it relies, first, on surprise: questioning on behalf of faith, hope and charity. Then follows an imperious demand that everyone should stop, repeated with increasing, staccato urgency. Finally, with the readers paying full attention, on go the brakes. The second question has the understanding, sympathetic tone of a disappointed auntie reasoning with a naughty child. The change of voice is achieved by the lively use of punctuation to control sentence length and separate the contrasting questions, one haughty and one matey, but both putting into words what the readers were thinking.

> Even at this time of triumph it is important to remember the verities of cricket between England and Australia. Winning is not what matters; the Ashes are about renewing old friendships in a spirit of sporting endeavour between two nations with a common bond. But, by God, isn't it great to beat the bastards?
> Matthew Engel, *Guardian*

The question is at the end but it's worth waiting for. Throughout it's the tone of voice that does it. At the start, mouthing plummy, treacly platitudes commonly employed to make defeat more acceptable: 'the verities of cricket' … 'winning is not what matters' … 'renewing old friendships in a spirit of sporting endeavour'. Then suddenly there's a whoop of joy as the writer scents blood: 'Isn't it great to beat the bastards?' Again, the punch word in the punch position.

> Do you have an annual appraisal system? Why? Before expending energy on a process so complicated and potentially controversial, it makes sense to ask what you hope to achieve. Most businesses do not know why they have one. They just do.
> *Accountancy*

Barristers, it's said, ask witnesses questions in court only when they know what the answer will be. Writers can't be certain how readers will reply. One device is the immediate follow-up question. The joy here is that whether the answer to the first is yes or no, the second question is still valid. Great final sentence, making the writer's point with the print equivalent of a despairing shrug of the shoulders.

5 Quote

The most controversial of intro types. Variously damned and dismissed as lazy and/or confusing for the reader, and typographically difficult for the designer and sub. In its favour: a good quote can be very effective and, if accompanied by a whopping big picture of the subject, it's a strange reader who would be confused. But best used sparingly.

> 'I think it's safe to say that no one has ever called Rupert Murdoch a tree hugger,' said Michael Bloomberg, the mayor of New York, in a speech the other day. Yet Murdoch had committed his companies 'to a major sustainability initiative' that would dramatically reduce their carbon emissions.
> Alexander Chancellor, Guardian

Opens with an entertaining quote. The reaction is to read on to mock (most Guardian readers?) or marvel. Then comes the shock: Murdoch is thinking about global warming. What is he up to?

> 'Sophisticated nursery food' is how Mark Hix, chef-director of Caprice Holdings, described the menu offering of the 60-year-old restaurant Le Caprice. 'It's not the kind of food you think long and hard about. You can eat it with a fork while you're doing business.'
> Tom Vaughan, Caterer and Hotelkeeper

One of the most famous old restaurants of London and here, from the chef-director's mouth, is the entertaining truth, valuable for b2b readers – a dead simple and highly effective way to keep a certain type of customer happy: think about their priorities and make life easy for them.

One way to start with a quote is just to leave out the quote marks.

> I'm getting a bit sick of your apoplectic roarings, wrote a male reader last week . . .
> Lynda Lee-Potter, Daily Mail

But the neatest way of dealing with the quote problem is to use reported speech: you avoid the technical difficulty but keep the immediacy of the spoken word.

> Gillian Helfgott, wife of the controversial pianist David Helfgott, says she doesn't give a hoot about the critics. Not a hoot. In fact she spends an hour

telling me she doesn't give a hoot. During which time it becomes quite clear that she gives many hoots. She loathes them, despises them, detests them, thinks them spineless, passionless, loveless, worthless. 'You tell me, who has done more for classical music, David Helfgott or the critics?' She jabs her finger into my chest. I don't have to think too hard about the answer.

It is midnight. It has been a long evening. But she is relentless. This is one tough cookie . . .
Stephen Moss, *Guardian*

Content

You've grabbed them with the intro. Now you've got to keep them reading. The care and effort that go into each word of the opening should continue through to the end.

Ways to write feature body copy are many, various and determined by the brief. All should include good, clear, lively writing whatever the subject and whatever the aim – colour, information, description, anecdotes, quotes, comment, analysis. . . . Other aspects covered here include practical advice on writing b2b copy, guidance for the innumerate on statistics and ways to improve wordplay.

Colour

Well-chosen specific words are sensuous. Because they have 'handles', ie are graspable, they reach readers in a way concepts don't. Here's a GP writing about poverty and violence in the East End of London. Correction, about his experience of poor and violent men and women. Correction, what he has seen, felt, heard, touched, smelt.

> When I came I didn't know what the bruised face of a raped heroin addict was like, or how children could be locked up without food, four in a room by a drunken father as a punishment, or what happens to a jaw when it is broken in a domestic fight and concealed. Now I do. I know what decomposed bodies of alcoholics smell like after two weeks, and the noises made when dying in pain and what happens to a woman's face when she is told her breast cancer has spread. I wish I didn't.
> David Widgery, *Guardian*

The rhythmic writing falls into two sections. First there's a powerful list of three – bruised face, locked-up children and broken jaw – followed by a short factual sentence: 'Now I do.' Next another list of three but all involving death – decomposed bodies, dying noises, woman's face, followed by a more passionate variation of the first coda: 'I wish I didn't.' The powerful images need no extra adjectives.

Even with much less sensational subjects, the advice about choosing concrete, graspable words is the secret of 'writing in pictures' because well-chosen words speak immediately and vividly to readers.

> It's 20 years since I've been in Moscow, since when the permafrost of the Soviet regime has melted and it's now possible to find a hotel without a concierge guarding each floor, but with plugs in the baths and a towel larger than a face flannel.
> Richard Eyre, *Guardian*

So much more powerful than 'vastly improved conditions'.

Information

Some features are planned to be fact-heavy and the details you include depend on your judgment of what's interesting to the readers. Readability depends on how you present those facts: loosely packed or indigestibly squashed. Take this description of the special effects for the film *Titanic*:

> Chief among them, of course, was a replica of the Titanic. Or rather several of them. Even a 1/20 scale model was over 45ft long. There was a 25ft version just to work out camera angles; there was one of the weed-encrusted wreck – which was hung upside down from a ceiling to make filming it easier. Shots of it were laced into shots of the real wreck.
>
> But the big ship, the one that counted, was built along a sandy strip of beach in Mexico, and it was, near as damn it, full-sized. It must have been an extraordinary sight to see its vast, weird outline riding the waterfront sands. The Titanic was, in its day, the largest moving object ever made. The reproduction can claim to be the largest film prop ever made. It was 775ft long – 90 per cent full size – and for obvious reasons it had to be made able to tilt.
>
> The real Titanic, best iron and steel as she was, couldn't take the weight of having her back end lifted out of the water; it broke as she sank so the reproduction had to be made stronger, because it had to be tilted and lowered dozens of times without real loss of life. Three-and-a-half million tons of steel and 15,000 sheets of plywood went into it . . .
> *Daily Mail* Weekend magazine

Fact-packed – more than 20 in the first two pars – but not dense. The writing is airy with hardly a backward reference or sub-clause before the subject. Most of the figures are round numbers, an aid to understanding in consumer writing. Exact numbers are wanted for b2bs, of course.

Even more packed and astonishing is this feature about a US champion eater. Most competitors are grossly overweight, but one of the most famous, Sonya Thomas, is surprisingly tiny, weighing around seven stone.

> To give some idea of this woman's unlikely ability, consider just some of the records she currently holds: 8.2lbs of chilli-and-cheese-covered French fries in ten minutes, 8.3lbs of Vienna Sausages in ten minutes, 552 oysters in ten minutes, 5.95lbs of meatballs in 12 minutes, 162 chicken wings in 12 minutes, 8.4lbs of baked beans in two minutes and 47 seconds, 80 chicken nuggets in five minutes, 8.6lbs of sweet potato casserole in 11 minutes and – just for those people who were impressed by Paul Newman's ability to put away 50 hard-boiled eggs in the movie *Cool Hand Luke* – she has also scoffed down 52 such eggs in five minutes. It took Newman's character all night. Last August in Harrington, Delaware, Sonya ate 40 crabcakes in 12 minutes. It is that record she is here this morning to defend, or rather, to break. She has a plan to make it happen. 'It's actually easier if you can dunk them in water,' she confides.
> *Independent*

Compulsive reading and all the more surprising because the first sentence is 112 words long, a length that usually guarantees turn-off. The readability of this giant sentence illustrates the point made elsewhere in this book: express similar ideas similarly; in other words avoid variation for the sake of it. The list works because it deals with graspable specifics: exactly how much food she ate, what kind of food she ate and how long it took her. Relentlessly, the stats pile up, with the info always presented in the same order: amount, food, time.

Resist the temptation to use bullet points here because though something would be won – probably an immediate appreciation of her gargantuan achievements – something would be lost: that uncomfortable feeling reached as the sentence ends, after fact after fact, stat after stat has piled up and the reader feels very bloated indeed.

Here's a b2b feature from *Drapers*, the fashion business magazine. It's their regular weekly 'Indicator' slot relating to sales and trends. The week's subject was shoes (footwear to *Drapers* readers).

> Women's mainstream footwear retailers are hedging their bets against a rainy spring next year, despite a positive week of trading. The independents surveyed for this week's 'Indicator' were holding back an average of 25% of their spring budget . . . until closer to the season.

> Following a pattern set at the Moda Footwear show this year, which saw fewer orders placed at the event as buyers held out to order as late as possible, retailers were playing it safe after a summer of downpours.

> Caroline Turner, owner of Caroline Turner Shoes in Middlesex, said: 'I wouldn't say I'm being cautious – I'm being prudent. It's good to have a

bit of flexibility. I've had a great season and I'm only going to hold back about 10%.'

At F. Dickinson Footwear in Barrow-in-Furness, Cumbria, owner Hannah Gummers agreed there was a lesson to be learnt. 'We've sold 60% of the sandals we sold last year, so we're going to buy much smaller next year. And if we have an unusually hot summer, we'll need to have a scout around to top up the stock.'

But business was not a total wash-out, with 42% of those surveyed finishing the week ahead of the same time last year, and only 18% reporting a drop of sales.

Drapers' meaty copy, spot-on for targeted readers, offering revealing stats, facts, reports and future plans, clearly fulfils the editorial policy of keeping readers up to date with the latest trends and quotes from named traders.

Now facts for consumers. Cleverly chosen practical information about the ten best British beaches selected for a variety of reasons – children, above all – is more convincing than loads of quotes. In this case the facts are exactly what parent readers want to know.

TORRE ABBEY SANDS, TORQUAY, DEVON

It's as though this large, sandy beach was designed with families in mind. Located right by the town centre of Torquay, it has plenty of parking, is close to the train station and just across the road from Torre Abbey Meadows parkland. Palm trees, evidence of the area's mild microclimate, give the approach to the beach a distinctly un-British, tropical feel.

The clincher: in a recent scientific study, Torquay beaches were found to be the best for sandcastle building, due to their extremely fine-grained sand which has superior cohesive powers.
Chris Elwell-Sutton, *RAC World*

Advice

Music Teacher, a trade magazine for music teachers and students, offers practical guidance to anyone starting orchestral work. Most orchestras – unless they are large enough to have their own library – hire the necessary sheet music. These scores, which musicians call 'hire parts', are often printed on poor paper and arrive tatty and defaced with almost indecipherable notes in a variety of languages. Nine aspects of best practice when marking up orchestral parts are described in this particular feature. The opening section is 'Equipment'.

Use a soft lead pencil – 2B is fine, but 4B even better. You will be able to write more clearly, more easily. Hard pencils (any H pencil, including HB) require more pressure to produce legible writing, and this can damage paper. Moreover, their fainter trace can be especially hard to read under the glare of concert hall lamps.

As well as a supply of spare pencils, keep a good quality artist's eraser. Pencil-end rubbers are fine for the occasional correction, but they wear out quickly under heavy use, and are more inclined to leave smears.

Never ever use ink.
Toby Deller, *Music Teacher*

Sound advice supplied with that truly valuable extra: reasons. These help to ensure that readers follow the advice and don't just go half-way, thinking 'Must take a pencil – but I haven't really time to go to the stationers, so any old one will do.'

Advice for swimming pool operators to protect their customers' safety is supplied for *Health Club Management*, a b2b magazine, by a barrister who successfully represented a lifeguard during an eight-week court case.

Be much more willing to clear the pool. It seems common practice to leave this as a last resort. Clear it early, as soon as you suspect all is not right, or you cannot effectively supervise the pool.

Ensure lifeguard training is carried out as recommended by HSG 179 and that your records are up-to-date.

Follow post-incident procedures. Be aware that what you say after the incident may be used against you.

Refuse to multi-task. Cleaning poolside, conducting pool tests and performing other duties while lifeguarding a pool could compromise the level of care you provide for bathers.
Health Club Management

Clearly, succinctly set out. Full of valuable 'must know' information.

Anecdotes

One good anecdote is worth loads of description. After his death, Robert Maxwell, one-time owner of the *Mirror*, was described as 'the 20th century's most monstrous confidence trickster – bully, braggart, liar, cheat, thief'. That's truly powerful writing, but surely the following anecdote – collected first-person and stored for years – is even more memorable:

Since everyone else recited their favourite Maxwell story last week, let me give you mine. Shortly after he dawn-raided the bankrupt British Printing Corporation in the early 1980s, I invited him to lunch in my office. Still persona non grata in the City after the DTI's [Department of Trade and Industry] savage condemnation of him, he was typically bouncing back and wanted bank support.

An hour before lunch he rang, down a suitably crackly line. 'I'm sorry I can't make your lunch,' he boomed. 'I'm in Bucharest.'

I said I was sorry to hear it, particularly as there were going to be some other interesting people there. Who were they, he inquired. Two bankers, I replied, Philip Wilkinson of NatWest and John Quinton of Barclays.

'You've got Wilkinson and Quinton, have you? Give me a moment.' The line went dead, then he was back on. 'I'll be round there in ten minutes.' And he was.
Ivan Fallon, *Sunday Times*

The anecdote swings along, describing what happened with no added frills except 'boomed' and 'suitably crackly', words which prove their value later. The end is beautifully judged. Good anecdotes require no editorialising.

When Kitty Kelley was researching her unauthorised biography of Frank Sinatra she was told the singer had bought $200,000 worth of furniture in cash in wrapping paper from a Las Vegas casino – an indication of Sinatra's links with the gaming industry.

She found a friend who bore a resemblance to Sinatra. Kelley then had her own hair done to match that of Sinatra's wife, Barbara. Together, Kelley and her friend went to the furniture store. They told the sales assistant that they had heard that Frank Sinatra had bought some furniture from the store. Indeed he had, said the salesman.

Well, said Kelley, they were so fond of the singer they modelled themselves on him, right down to their looks and lifestyle. They had to have the same furniture for their home, which was an exact copy of his. What did he buy? The proud salesman rattled off the list. We will take it, said Kelley. Because we follow his life to the letter, we must pay the way he did – so how did he pay? Which credit card did he use?

The salesman produced the payslip. Cash. Come on, honey, said Kelley, clutching her companion, we must go to Las Vegas and get the cash. They left the store and never returned. She had her story . . .
Chris Blackhurst, *Independent on Sunday*

The style here is speech reported, a device which enables the reader to hear the conversation as it might have happened, rather than reported speech ('Kelley then told the salesman that they were devoted fans of Sinatra, modelling their appearance and lifestyle on him and would like to obtain the same furniture that he had bought').

Short anecdotes can be equally telling. From an obit of Violet Carlson, the Broadway dancer:

She once broke her wrist playing in the Jerome Kern musical *Sweet Adeline*, had it set in plaster and was back on stage before the end of the performance.
Guardian

Here's a long-remembered anecdote about the combative cricketer Ian Botham:

> By the time he was two, Ian had already emerged as an uncompromising competitor. 'We had organised a short race among navy children,' his mother recalls. 'Ian wasn't much of a sprinter in those days but this time he got out in front. Near the finishing line he turned and knocked down the other children, one by one, and finished the race by himself.'
> Dudley Doust, *Sunday Times* Magazine

No surprise then that some 20 years later Ian Botham was hurling bouncers at the Aussies.

Quotes

What people say brings vitality to copy, relieves solid text, changes pace and offers a fresh or authoritative voice, allowing the interviewee to speak. In most features a quote early on acts as a 'kicker', enlivening serious introductions or detailed scene-setting.

Unlike news reporters, who attribute quotes at the beginning or end of the sentence, feature writers – as ever – have more choice. They can break up the quote to show it to best advantage. The placing of 'she says', below, enables the strongest words to occupy the most important position in the sentence.

> 'The foot,' she says, 'is an architectural masterpiece.'
> *Financial Times*

Writers can animate an ordinary quote with description, movement and colour, which act like stage directions.

> 'If I was doing a 30-second piece to camera right now,' says the twinkly, rumpled man sprawled on the park bench, 'I would get into a completely obsessed state. No really, that's true.' He sits up and leans forward, insistent. 'I'm as nervous now, before every single thing I do, as I was the day I did my first piece of television.'
>
> It is hard to think of a less plausible thing for David Dimbleby to say . . .
> Decca Aitkenhead, *Guardian*

When a quote is less than hoped for, context can give meaning.

> Did she use memories of her father's death to help her performance? 'Yes, I did. Of course. You draw on whatever you have,' she says briskly. Silence. I can see her wondering if there isn't something more urgent she should be doing . . .
> Kristin Scott Thomas interviewed in the *Sunday Times* Magazine

Using other writers' quotes lifted from cuts can make a not-so-astonishing comment splendid. This is how Bernard Levin, long ago but memorably, greeted the news that Humphrey Searle's *Hamlet* was to be performed in Covent Garden:

> The news is welcome, even though from what I have heard of Mr Searle's music I am inclined to react as Beachcomber did when he read the news that someone (Janacek, actually) had written an opera to Dostoievsky's *The House of the Dead*. 'Stap me,' said the sage, 'I warrant there'll be some lilting tunes in *that* work.'

Questionnaires are a specialised form of feature where the interviewee (or their PR) does the work and gets the credit. Could that be why questionnaires are often disparaged by journalists? Studying the better examples provides a great guide to using quotes, shortened and pointed to maximum effect.

> *What's the worst piece of gossip you've ever read about yourself?*
>
> The *Sun* once listed '20 Things You Didn't Know About Barry Norman' and there were at least ten things that I didn't know about Barry Norman.
> Barry Norman, *Empire*
>
> *What would you like written on your tombstone?*
>
> Unavailable. Please try me on the mobile.
> Mel Smith, *Empire*

Comment

Lynn Barber's interview with a famous and elderly film star starts with a warning that the interview is taking a long, long, long time. She loves words and to push the message home dextrously uses one that has two meanings: one serious, one facetious. A joyful judgment – you'll know it when you reach it.

> It isn't as if he's particularly, preternaturally boring. I mean probably by the standards of veteran Hollywood stars, he's in the upper percentile of interest. It is just that he suffers from anecdotage, the terrible brain rot that overcomes elderly people who have spent a large portion of their lives on chat shows. When you ask him a question he quickly scans it for a cue word, feeds the cue word into his memory files, and then, zap, brings out an anecdote that has the cue word in it. Being an actor, he of course delivers his anecdote with every possible nuance of expression, animation, funny voices, gestures, pauses for suspense, which makes it take about an hour longer than it's worth.
> Lynn Barber, *Independent on Sunday*

More shrewd assessment. Tennis star Roger Federer answers 17 questions from Sarah Shephard of *Sport* magazine as efficiently as he plays. At the very end of the interview, after the last question, is a single word that says it all – and it isn't one of Federer's.

Question: As both a man and a tennis player, what is your view on the female players receiving equal pay in tennis when they only play three sets?

[Squirms] 'I don't mind it. Honestly, it's OK . . .'

Oh, the power of well-chosen verbs: says it all.

Editors and features editors rarely include passion as one of the qualities they look for in feature writing. That may be because the image of the tough, cynical, detached journalist lives on. But editors certainly rate it when they get it. The following feature was remembered years after it first appeared.

Women and children sleep two to a bed. Others sleep on the kitchen floor and in the sitting-room. There are about 120 people in a house suitable for 36. It is like moving from one sort of hell to another, said a social worker.

That's one view of Chiswick Women's Aid Centre, Erin Pizzey's refuge for battered wives, which faces a crisis following Hounslow council's decision to withdraw part of its £10,000 urban aid grant unless it complies with regulations on fire, health and overcrowding.

Erin Pizzey and colleague Ann Ashby say they will go to jail rather than comply with the regulations. . . . They will not end their policy of running the Chiswick centre as an open-door refuge.

Ann Ashby reports the case of a woman who arrived a few nights ago: 'Her husband had pulled her trousers down and poured boiling water between her legs. He'd beaten her about so she had six broken ribs as well, and bruises and cuts all over. Her children were suffering too. She came to us, we took her to hospital and brought her back with us. She can stay as long as she likes. You can't expect us to turn a woman like that away.'
Carol Dix, *Guardian*

The woman's story is told without the use of any judgmental language. The reader is free to decide. Calmly presented facts out-perform paragraphs of emotional ranting. The same goes for simple statistics.

China executes more people each year than the rest of the world put together. Methods include lethal injection and firing squad. Amnesty knows of at least 1,010 executions in China in 2006, but a Chinese legal scholar estimates that about 8,000 people are executed each year – 22 people a day. There are 68 crimes punishable by death in China, two-thirds of them non-violent crimes.
Amnesty Magazine

Statistics

To be used intelligently. Feature writers may be literate, but far too many, alas, are innumerate. They've become journalists because they were 'good at English and bad at maths', says Roy Greenslade, once of the *Mirror* and now of City University. The result is that they're impressed by the numerate and tend to trust any statistics they're given. Quite simply, they don't check the maths or use their common sense. The *Guardian* admits printing more than 80 corrections relating to numbers within a period of six months.

Worse than appearing in the *Guardian*'s 'Corrections and clarifications' section are mistakes revealed in letters to the editor.

> To the *Times*
>
> You state that '134 carrier bags per person in the UK per year would cover the planet twice over'. My calculation says that, if so, each carrier bag would have to be about 360×360 metres, or about half a million times larger than the ones I get. Waste is a problem, but let's not blow it out of proportion.
>
> Charles Armitage, London SW6
>
> To the *Independent*
>
> Something is rotten in the toilet statistics department of the *Independent*. If Nick Allen was impressed by the number of years Britons fritter evacuating their bowels he must have been even more astonished at the extraordinary daily catharsis apparently achieved by the Chinese. According to your article on Chinese economic ascendancy, 1.3 billion Chinese produce 3.7 billion tons of sewage a day, an eye-watering 2.8 tons each. I had been worrying about Chinese goods flooding global markets but it seems a more awful deluge is about to overwhelm us.
>
> Tom Mitchell, Surrey

Editors and readers value statistics because they come cloaked with authority. PRs know this well and so do politicians. In all cases, check. Don't accept statistics at face value. Think, question and use a calculator whenever necessary. If you're unsure, double-check, go back to the source, get help from a statistician or contact an organisation such as the Office for National Statistics or the Royal Statistical Society.

It's important to know the numbers involved in any research (over 2,000 participants are needed to achieve +/– 3 per cent accuracy); also to know the relevant definitions used. There's a theory that dubious figures sometimes come from pressure groups. For example, one much quoted 'fact' is that one woman in five suffers domestic violence. This figure is apparently based on using a definition of 'domestic violence' as being 'forced to do menial and trivial tasks'. 'By that token,' concludes one critic, 'almost everyone in a relationship is abused.'

Sometimes figures can provide a feature on their own. These 'statistics' were reproduced in *Private Eye*'s 'Street of Shame' column while the Mills/McCartney divorce was at the pre-court stage:

£20 million – Heather Mills-McCartney's divorce, according to the *Telegraph*
£30 million – Heather Mills-McCartney's divorce, according to the *Sun*
£50 million – Heather Mills-McCartney's divorce, according to the *Express*
£70 million – Heather Mills-McCartney's divorce, according to the *Mail*

Wordplay[2]

Features editors are shrewd and practised judges. They read for a living day in, day out, and quickly recognise writing that needs substantial work or can be improved by a few swift changes. They welcome work that's lively, writing that's stylish. But they rejoice when they find a feature by a clever writer who can play with words.

> Wanting to meet a writer because you like their books is like wanting to meet a duck because you like pâté.
> Margaret Atwood, *Guardian*

> He [a politician] also oozes sincerity; his brow is so furrowed, you could throw a handful of seeds over it, and in three months' time you'd probably have a good show of green beans . . .
> Rachel Cooke, *Observer*

> I've always thought that journalism is such a loathsome profession that our coat of arms ought to be emblazoned with two maggots rampant over a bucket of sick, surmounted by a chequebook.
> Victor Lewis-Smith, *Mirror*

Three examples. The first, an unexpected, unreal comparison that's a powerful put-down. This works by choosing a word that's totally unexpected but linked verbally. For example, commenting on a politician who is quoted as 'wishing to run the country', by adding: 'I wouldn't let him run my bath.'

The second example is a crazy visual suggestion that works by ridiculous exaggeration. P G Wodehouse was a master of this. 'Roderick Spode? Big chap with a small moustache and the sort of eye that can open an oyster at sixty paces.'

In the third example horrible, repulsive yet memorable images are topped off powerfully by the sardonic introduction of money with its corrupting, debasing effects.

Not every writer has a naturally clever way with words. The most able are often those who read extensively and compulsively as children. For those who are interested, some 'clever writing' can be developed with practice. A great deal rests on the ability to conjure surprising visual comparisons, turning reality or famous quotes upside down or substituting one item or idea for another.

2 See also Chapter 8, 'Style', page 150.

Francis Beckett is the kind of biographer whose subjects find him either at their feet or at their throat.
Michael White, *Guardian*

This works by the simple means of writing in pictures (feet and throat) rather than the expected conceptual non-visual words (praising or criticising).

a master of evasion, more slippery than a Jacuzzi full of KY jelly.
Richard Littlejohn, *Sun*

This description of Michael Shea, one-time press secretary to the Queen, uses a clever visual metaphor to get across that slippery judgment.

The television programme *Together Again* featured couples reunited after having broken up.

What eventually emerged through the fog of cigarette smoke and psycho-babble was the classic tale of a man who drinks to forget that he's stupid and violent, thereby becoming a stupid, violent drunk, and although he finished by promising to go on the wagon, I fear that what he really needed was a brain operation. Not a lobotomy or a leucotomy though. Just an operation to have one put in.
Victor Lewis-Smith, *Evening Standard*

This fresh twist, following what appeared to be suggesting a known operation, makes a wholly different and telling point.

A prime minister supports (?) his successor:

The words were warm but the body language was awful. He [Blair] umm'ed and ah'ed. His eyes flickered wildly.

'I am absolutely delighted to, um, give my full support to Gordon. As. The next leader of the Labour party. And – er – prime minister . . .' It got worse. His teeth were so gritted you could use them on a snow-covered motorway.
Simon Hoggart, *Guardian*

Two destructive pars that ridicule the then prime minister's body language. The first starts with judgmental scene-setting. Then his speech is cruelly deconstructed, using punctuation to transform and mock what was said. The full points – and dashes – reluctantly . . . stutter home the kill. The final unflattering and visual metaphor . . . how much lower could it go? Guillotine writing.

The flood of complaints following TapeHead's comments on Richard E. Grant's performance in *The Scarlet Pimpernel* continues unabated. How, the cry goes up, could you be so lenient?
Jim Shelley, *Guardian*

Old but wonderful: memorable and telling, the vicious and exact opposite of what a reader expects.

Detail

Using one fact to embody a person or trend is especially valuable for short features, but the detail must tell. From a feature on the retiring head of American Airlines:

> A fierce cost-cutter who once saved $100,000 by removing olives from all AA's salads . . .
> Economist

Case histories

Case histories are probably the easiest way to cover a complex subject in a hurry. They're quicker to write because there's no need for cross-weaving or smooth links. Another plus: the people interviewed are usually happier because they have a section all to themselves, as in this feature about couples married at Chelsea register office. Combining all seven stories into one feature would destroy the uniqueness of each couple.

DAVID LANGLEY AND REBECCA SWAINSTON

> The odds were stacked against David Langley, 32, and Rebecca Swainston, 35, meeting at all. He is a lecturer in performing arts and was drafted in at the eleventh hour to drive a minibus of teachers to the open-air opera in Holland Park last summer. For the first time in his life he walked out of a performance and stumbled over Rebecca sitting on the steps. 'She spotted the bottle of Chablis in my hand and asked if she could have a sip. We sat and talked and I immediately knew I wanted to marry her. I proposed four weeks later in the Alhambra in Granada, and when she'd stopped crying she said yes.'
>
> All their friends were amazed. 'I was the last person on earth who was going to get married. I enjoyed my freedom and thought love was for poets and priestesses,' reveals David.
>
> From the register office the couple and their guests took a red London bus to a humanist ceremony and reception for 200 people in the Duke of York's Headquarters on the Kings Road. Throughout the reception slides of David and Rebecca, from the age of one, were projected onto the walls. After their big day, the couple travelled to Florence for a three-week honeymoon.
> Jane Simms, London Magazine

One way to celebrate an anniversary is to mark each of the number of years achieved with a matching story. Here, among the 30 greatest characters chosen to mark the thirtieth anniversary of *Star Wars*, is C-3PO:

> You may think the *Star Wars* character you most resemble is Han Solo or Boba Fett or, if you lack self-esteem, Mouse Robot but – look into your

heart – you know it's C-3PO. He's smart (six million languages), loyal (it is his intervention that saves Artoo at the Jawa sale-yard), sensitive, occasionally says the wrong thing at the wrong time but always has his heart in the right place (he offers to donate his circuits to his battered-up friend). C-3PO is redolent of *Star Wars'* unique (especially at the time) ability to warm up the coldest staples of science-fiction. In jettisoning his original perception of Threepio as a used-car salesman for Anthony Daniels' perfectly pitched prissy English butler, Lucas turned a robot into *Star Wars'* most recognisably human character, marked by universal doubts and everyday frailties. Doesn't that sound a bit like you?

DEFINING MOMENT Wandering around in the no-man's land of Tatooine, bemoaning his fate. Quintessential Threepio.
Ian Freer, *Empire*

Warm, affectionate, evocative and persuasive writing – provided you love *Star Wars*, that is.

Endings

Readers who find a feature's first par mildly interesting often sample the end before deciding whether to read the rest, so the last par grows in importance. A well-crafted ending rewards both the hooked and the 'dip in' reader by offering a satisfying conclusion, nailing the feature down firmly. Don't fall into the essay or speech trap by repeating the intro, but an echo of it can be telling.

Features often end with statements or quotes; less commonly with anecdotes and descriptions; rarely with questions. Whatever the approach chosen, it should suit the feature, reader and publication. Concluding statements, for example, can be positive, negative, tentative even. They can hammer or thump home a point. What they should avoid is being timid or apologetic, slinking away out of sight.

The *Mirror*'s feature about Sir Alex Ferguson's dressing-room doctrine (page 51) ends with a neat Fergie quote which encapsulates his practical philosophy:

> But the most important thing is to play a team that wins.

Often the most effective conclusions echo the start but show the reader clearly how much progress has been achieved, how much ground has been covered. Probably more than anywhere else in a feature, knowing about power points in a sentence pays off. The most forceful endings put the most important word at the end, in the final 'punch' position.

The feature by Sally Brampton (page 54) ends:

But what pleases me most is that, for one whole year, I have not wanted to die. It sounds absurd but every morning when I wake up, I feel proud.

I am still here.

A feature starting:

My first instinct was that Judy Hall was barking mad. My second was that I would be, too, if I didn't get out of there as quickly as possible.

ends:

I don't know, but as I drove away across the Wiltshire Downs I felt lighter and less sceptical than I had been four hours earlier. A ghost had been laid to rest.
Annabel Heseltine, *Daily Mail*

Again, a huge change. The writer, who wanted to get out as quickly as possible in the intro, stayed for four hours and left with changed perceptions.

Endings work well when they embody some conclusion reached during the course of the story that is of help to the reader. The intro to the following feature about libel lawyers starts with an analogy that all but the smuggest swot can identify with.

Watching your editor read a solicitor's letter threatening libel is like watching your parents read your school report. You may have goofed, but don't panic – unless the letter is from [five law firms mentioned].

It ends:

If more publishers had a bit of guts, a lot of these threatening letters could be stopped dead.

The feature included the information that there were a total of possibly 100 lawyers expert in libel law and that almost all solicitors' letters were uninformed posturing. Reassuring and helpful.

Here's the conclusion to the intro on page 56 about staff appraisal, in a magazine designed for busy top-level accountants.

Appraisal systems are the last ditch attempt by personnel to get managers to do some (people) managing. The problem is that they give managers an excuse not to do it the rest of the year. The answer is not to spend money and time on useless systems but to insist that managers manage – and that they are willing, able and motivated to give objective, timely and helpful feedback to their staff appropriate to their level of readiness. Spend the personnel manager's time on reinforcing this, not on collecting bits of paper.
Accountancy

This ending could achieve stage 4 on the feature scale (see page 43) and produce positive action.

Readers interested but not hooked by the intro to a feature about John Updike, describing how he'd forgotten the number of his hotel room, might decide to check by scanning the last par.

> As I stand up to go, he does too, and abruptly catches sight of his underpants. 'Oh God,' he cries, scooping them up and feverishly stuffing them, with a pair of worn black socks, into his suitcase. 'How careless of me. I do hope it's not psychic litter.'

What was going on? Back to the intro at once.

Extras

Back stories, stats boxes, sidebars, tables and panels may look like afterthoughts but they're now integral to many features. Most writers need to think about them, if not at the idea stage then during research.

Content and style are determined by readers' interests and the time they have to spare. For extras, writing should be more concise than usual, at times telegrammatic even. Easy reading is the key: short subject–verb–object sentences. Even subject–object phrases. Clauses should be kept to a minimum.

Journalists often give PRs a hard time, bludgeoning them for immediate help and offering scant thanks. Here's where courtesy and consideration pay off, as PRs are able to do much of the labour-intensive work, providing info for extras that might otherwise take lengthy dredging.

Just facts

> Scandinavian Kitchen, 61 Great Titchfield, W1W 7PP (020 7580 7161/ www.scandikitchen.co.uk) Oxford Circus tube. Open Mon–Fri 8am–7pm, Sat 10am–6pm, Sun 10am–4pm. Lunch for one with coffee and cake: around £7.

Nothing but relevant information, clearly punctuated. After accuracy, the most important thing to remember in boxes is intelligent punctuation. 'Opening times 10am–noon, 2pm–4pm Monday–Tuesday, early closing Wednesday 10am–noon, Saturdays 9am–4pm.' Any more of that and readers will be lost. Here's where full stops, dashes and semi-colons prove their worth.

Collected and selected

An impressive 11-page special on Everest in *Sport* featured fact boxes.

FAST FACTS SOUTHEAST RIDGE ROUTE

From Nepal
Base camp Khumbu Glacier
First completed 1953
Popularity 800 out of 1,318 ascents by the end of 2000
Main season April/May
Cost of commercial expedition $40,000 to $75,000
Duration 60–70 days
Natural hazards Avalanches, crevasses, sub-zero temperatures, hurricane-force winds, icefalls, sheer drops

There was also a page dedicated to what happens to the body at the summit. Not attractive.

> Lack of oxygen to the brain reduces the mental capacity of climbers to that of a small child. Near the summit, the brain loses thousands of cells a minute. In this condition, poor decision-making leads to fatal mistakes. Hallucinations and paralysis through fear are possible.
> *Sport*

Large quantities of information: boxes and panels

A *Horse* magazine interview with owners of a livery stable, three of whose horses died after eating acorns, had five 'extras':

- fact box on the likelihood of horses dying from eating poisonous plants, including avoiding action owners could take
- illustrated panels of 14 mildly toxic, toxic and fatal plants (Yew example below)
- fact box on ragwort, the commonest cause of poisoning; where to obtain free information
- small par offering free info on revitalising grazing from a specialist organisation
- small par on the forthcoming second edition of a book on equine nutrition and feeding.

Yew

Appearance: Evergreen shrub or small tree, reaching 20m and living for up to 1,500 years. Reddish bark, dark needle-like leaves, small yellow bead-like (male) or green pear-shaped (female) flowers in March and bright red hollow-ended berries in late September.

Habitat: Parks, churchyards, broad-leaved woods and chalk down-lands.

Effect: Muscle tremors, unco-ordination, nervousness, difficulty in breathing, diarrhoea, convulsions, collapse and heart failure.

Toxin: Taxmine, a potent alkaloid.

HORSE WARNING: A horse eating as little as 0.05% of his bodyweight will prove fatal.

Valuable, practical information for the horse-mad readership.

Speed-read summary boxes

Despite having the most educated readers in terms of years spent studying, doctors' magazines often have features with bullet-point boxes in large type which repeat the main findings boiled down to a few sentences. These are the journalistic equivalent of 'executive summary' pars designed for hyper-busy readers.

Key points

- Conservative therapy in the form of physiotherapy by an experienced and interested physiotherapist is the first-line management of GSI.
- Burch colposuspension can give a 90 per cent objective cure rate and is the current 'gold standard' surgical treatment for GSI.
- Continence devices may be useful in the short term in women awaiting surgery or in the longer term in those not suitable for or who do not wish to undergo surgery.
- Newer surgical techniques may offer less invasive treatment but careful appraisal is needed before they are adopted universally.

Pulse

Stat boxes

The best way to make stats readable is to delete verbs, adjectives, adverbs, prepositions and pronouns, and put what remains under relevant headings.

Autocar's section entitled 'Number crunching' includes stats on the following subjects to back up the earlier reviews of their featured cars:

- engine
- power and torque
- chassis and body
- transmission
- suspension
- steering
- brakes
- cabin noise

- safety
- green rating
- acceleration
- acceleration in gear
- max speeds in gear
- depreciation, compared over four years with two comparable cars.

Here's one of the lists: info about the Nissan X-Trail's economy performance:

TEST	Average	29.9mpg
	Touring	38.2mpg
	Track	15.5mpg
CLAIMED	Urban	30.4mpg
	Extra-urban	44.8mpg
	Combined	38.2mpg
	Tank size	65 litres
	Test range	428 miles

Impressive, added-value info.

Bullet-point boxes in b2bs

Depending on the complexity of the subject, features designed to include helpful facts can often look and read 'slabby'. This type of feature benefits from add-on bullet point extras, as do less complex features where extra advice boosts value.

A feature for teachers about body language in the classroom included add-ons on clothes to wear, style tips and the messages colours send out.

- Red: aggression, danger or warning (think the emergency services)
- Black: mournful or foreboding (think funeral)
- Green: calm (as in nature and often used in hospital wards)
- Blue: inspires confidence (cooling, such as fresh air or the sea)
- Yellow: cheerful, inviting and comfortable (the reason why fish aimed at children is often covered in yellow breadcrumbs)
- Grey: drab or boring (the colour of old age)
- Orange: enthusiasm and vibrancy (think beautiful sunrises or sunsets)
- Purple: dignity and power (regal implications).
TES Magazine

Info boxes

Straightforward value-added specialist information from experts:

Olympus' SuperSonic Wave Drive image stabilisation system uses motion sensors to shift the sensor in response to camera shake, the former cancelling

out the latter, but it's a mechanical system unlike electronic noise-reduction on, say, a pair of headphones. Because it's built into the camera body, lenses can be designed smaller and lighter, and long-time Olympus users will be pleased to hear it will also work with older OM system optics via an adaptor.
Photography Monthly

Sidebars to make a point

Just after his 'cancer of bent and twisted journalism' speech, a feature about Jonathan Aitken – the disgraced politician and former journalist who later went to prison for perjury – appeared in the *Journalist*. Alongside was this simple sidebar:

NUJ CODE OF CONDUCT – CLAUSE 2
A journalist shall at all times defend the principle of the freedom of the press and other media in relation to the collection of information and expression of comment and criticism. He/she shall strive to eliminate distortion, news suppression and censorship.
Journalist

After all this 'How to' . . . a reminder – always check. Always.

The details of Derek Malcolm's new book [page 5, G2, January 18] were correct except for the title, publisher and price. The book is *A Century of Films: Derek Malcolm's Personal Best* (not *Derek Malcolm's Personal Best: A Century of Films*). The publisher's name is IB Tauris (not ID Tauris), but more specifically, the imprint is Tauris Parke Paperbacks. The price is £9.99 not £9.95.

Yes, always check.

More on structure

Nub and context pars

Features have a beginning, a middle and an end. In simple ones the intro or hook leads straight on to a paragraph which lets the reader know exactly what the feature's about. This is commonly called the nub or 'dear reader' par.

But what if the feature is to investigate the financial difficulties of Nicaragua or explain new developments in leasehold property law in Scotland or demonstrate the results of taxation inequalities on booze between England and France – all of which, stated like that, make unappealing hooks? A link must be forged between the hook and the nub par. Enter the context par, setting out any necessary background.

Links

At all stages of writing, the way to ensure a feature flows smoothly is to go back to the top and read it aloud to yourself to check that nothing is ambiguous or mystifying, that sentences are not too long and that the rhythm is there.

How to link is a much disputed area. Smoothly flowing copy is one thing; lousy links are another, very off-putting.

Simple to complex

Here are examples of structure, from simple to complex, starting with a first-person story, simply but dramatically told. The hook is a reconstruction of an armed robbery, followed by the nub par, clarification and confirmation that the hold-up had a terrifying after-shock.

Hook:

> Blink. He is wearing a black polo-neck and a black mask with slits for eyes. The end of a double-barrelled shotgun is inches from my eyes. He knows as well as I do that the glass between us isn't bullet-proof. My life doesn't flash before me but I see a clear picture of my daughter being told her mum is dead. That's all I can think of. Blink.

Nub par:

> The flashbacks were horribly vivid. When a stranger points a shotgun at your face they're in control and you are left floundering. I floundered for two-and-a-half years. Every day I lost more control, and when I slept my dreams were full of monsters.

Start of main body copy. First section, retelling the event:

> It was just after 10am on a December day . . . at a sub-branch of Barclays in Leeds where I worked behind the cash desk. There had been two attempted robberies in the past two months and both times I was shocked but seemed to recover. The previous robbers had seemed amateurish – when I refused to hand over the money they ran.

> The third time was different. The bank was empty and I first saw the robbers when they were outside, running towards the entrance. They were wearing donkey jackets and black polo necks, with masks tucked into their collars. It was at that point that I pressed the silent alarm.

> As they ran through the doors they pulled sawn-off shot guns from their jackets. After I emptied the tills one of the two men said, 'Get the big stuff

or you're going to get hurt.' We have small cash limits in the till but they wanted the big bundles of notes which were on a time-delay lock.

When they realised they were not going to get what they'd come in for they began to look agitated. A customer walked in, saw what was happening and screamed. The one who had the gun pointing at me turned to the other and shouted 'get her' but she ran off. They must have realised the game was up, because they ran out of the building to their car. The police arrived minutes after they had left.

Second section: the consequences with specific details:

After the robbery I developed this irrational fear that the robbers would come back and get me. I started having nightmares in the form of flashbacks – but it was not only when I slept. It could be just when I closed my eyes.

I became very remote and territorial: it was *my* couch, it was *my* half of the bed. I stopped showing any emotions to my family. I reasoned that if they didn't love me as much they wouldn't miss me when I was killed. Once when Emma, my 10-year-old daughter, fell off her horse, I couldn't cuddle her. Can you imagine what I felt like?

Third section: hope dawns:

After two-and-half years a friend told me about a programme at Long Lartin prison in the Vale of Evesham where psychologists were bringing victims into contact with perpetrators. I phoned the prison and said I wanted to go the next day. I'd reached a point when it was less horrible to face my fears than allow them to spiral out of control.

Walking into Long Lartin was a pivotal moment in my life. I was expecting the armed robbers there to be the evil monsters of my nightmares, but they weren't. As I started to talk about my experience I realised I was regaining control. They had to listen to what I'd been through. When the day ended I felt relief. I went home and slept and have never had trouble sleeping since. And, at 33 years old, my family life is back to normal . . .

Armed robbers are top of the pecking order in prison and will say their crime is victimless and paid for by institutions that can afford it. When they are forced to see that they traumatise innocent people in the process, some become very emotional, some even cry.

Working up to the conclusion: surprise, this isn't another first-person 'TOTTY' (Triumph over Tragedy):

I am lucky because Barclays has seconded me to my current post – working in prisons making criminals consider the human cost of their violence – and has agreed to pay my salary for a year.

The fact that it's taken so long to mention Barclays gives hope the ghostwriter is not in the bank's pay. The ending shows progress, too, in a change in the writer's attitude to prisoners.

I still get emotional, even though the nightmares have gone. It was an event that changed my life and the way I think about criminals. I used to be a bang-them-up-with-bread-and-water person, now I believe in rehabilitation. I've never met the men who robbed my branch, but I know where they are and the sentences they are serving. I'll never forgive them, but I meet so many armed robbers that they've just become two of many.
Big Issue

Now a hook that turns into a context par:

'Why in France are there no campuses worthy of the name, no sports grounds, and another extraordinary thing: no libraries that open on Sundays?' Thus Nicolas Sarkozy on his country's sclerotic universities. For an ambitious president, these might seem modest goals. But it is a measure of the universities' dire condition that they seem revolutionary. France has 82 universities, teaching 1.5m students. All are public; none charges tuition fees; undergraduate enrolment charges are a tiny €165 ($220). All lecturers are civil servants. Universities cannot select students, who can apply only to ones near them.

The results speak for themselves. Not a single French university makes it into the world's top 40 . . .
Economist

Starts with a dramatic question voiced by the French president, using graspable examples – campuses, sports grounds and libraries – to illustrate what's wrong.

Only then does the writer introduce the 'context info': eight worrying statistics and unimpressive facts. To see how well the 'people first' approach works, start reading in line 6: 'France has 82 universities, teaching 1.5m students.' Pretty stodgy. Then go back to the original version to see how welcome those stats are after you've been introduced to the dire conditions under which the students learn.

Below is a *Financial Times* feature, this time about important concerns which were *not* being discussed in the imminent Netherlands general election. Hardly a great gripper, so the feature starts with a lively descriptive/narrative hook, involving a corny play on the word 'fit'.

Wim Kok, the Dutch prime minister, tugged manfully at a rowing machine. Fritz Bolkenstein and Jaap de Hoop Scheffer, his two main rivals, respectively wielded a tennis racquet and jogged on a treadmill. At an event convened last month by the country's heart foundation, each wanted to show he was fit for government.

Context pars follow:

Fitness in the eyes of the voters will be decided in a general election today. This follows a campaign which has by no means quickened the national pulse.

> As a series of inconclusive televised debates wound up and photo opportunities dwindled, the lunchtime news on the state-owned network yesterday devoted not a moment to domestic or European politics.

The nub par follows: this is what the feature is about and why the reader should read on.

> But the choice the Dutch will make . . . will help determine the economic course of a core participant in the union. And electoral sentiment is shifting leftward.

Main body copy follows. Four sections for each party:

> prospects for the left-wing parties
> prospects for the free-market liberals
> prospects for the right-wing parties
> coalition possibilities.

Conclusion: Kok's efforts bolster his chances.

Constructed carefully

Now for a fairly complex feature based on several interviews and detailed research. It's about two teams preparing to battle it out at the *University Challenge* final.

It's a good story, well told. In order to preserve a realistic 'read through', the whole feature is printed here without comment, though paragraphs that play a significant part in the structure are numbered to facilitate later examination.

> [1] Only a year ago, they were a laughing stock after slumping to the biggest defeat in the history of TV's *University Challenge*.

> Crushed by 360 points to 40, Birkbeck College, London, found themselves the butt of student bar jibes and even elicited the sympathy of normally hard-nosed quizmaster Jeremy Paxman.

> [2] Sixteen months on, however, things could not be more different.

> On Tuesday night on BBC2, after the greatest comeback in the show's 36-year history, Birkbeck will lock brains with reigning champions Magdalen College, Oxford . . .

> And the four-strong team are determined finally to bury the memory of that humiliation at the hands of Manchester University.

> Captain Mark Conway said: 'Getting to the final has been an achievement but our greatest challenge is yet to come. We would like to silence all the critics who had a go at Birkbeck's performance in the last series.'

> [3] Birkbeck is Britain's largest college for part-time students and all the *University Challenge* team combine full-time work with their studies.

Mr Conway, studying Classical Civilisation, is a teacher. Catherine Arbuthnott (Mediaeval Latin) a university administrator. Mike Austin (History and Archaeology) a chartered engineer and Neil Best (Art History) a bookseller.

Conway, 39, oversaw the recruitment of the current team. His predecessor as captain, David Allen, a maths student and trades union worker, had simply picked those who responded first to posters placed around the college.

[4] This year the selection process was far more rigorous.

Mike Austin, at 61 the squad's elder statesman, came forward after watching the excruciating previous year defeat. 'I just thought I could do better than that,' said Austin, who has provided a science dimension to a team made up of arts students.

All applications were thoroughly tested first. Then, when the team had been chosen, a secret weapon was devised to help them train – a mock-up of the famous *University Challenge* desk complete with the all-important buzzers.

To re-create the tension of the *University Challenge* studio, it was set up in Birkbeck's student union bar.

Test questions were fired at the team as fellow undergraduates stood around drinking beer and jeering at every fluffed question.

'It really helped sharpen us up – speed to the buzzer is the key to winning *University Challenge*,' said Miss Arbuthnott, a cousin of the Scottish aristocrat Viscount Arbuthnott. Yet despite many hours of practice, she admitted the shadow of last year's disaster loomed large as they went into the first round against Cardiff University.

[5] 'At one point we got stuck on 20 points and we were just praying we could get at least 45 points,' she said. But they went on to win and followed up with convincing victories against Robinson College, Cambridge, and Edinburgh.

The semi-final against Nottingham University was a tetchy affair. 'They were very smug and thought they would walk all over us. When they lost they couldn't even bear to shake our hands,' said Mr Austin.

[6] The final will be an intriguing contest of town versus gown.

Birkbeck, part of London University, was founded in 1832 at the Crown and Anchor Tavern in the Strand, when it was agreed to establish a 'London Mechanics Institution'.

The college – motto In Nocte Consillium, 'teaching by night' – is based in drab buildings in Central London and has spent the past decade staving off a series of financial crises.

By contrast, the Magdalen College team attend one of the oldest and wealthiest colleges in the country.

Its buildings include a historic tower, an ornate 15th Century banqueting hall and a chapel which is home to the famous Magdalen choristers and adorned with great art works including a Leonardo Da Vinci.

Magdalen alumni include Edward VIII, Princess Diana's brother, Earl Spencer, the historian A.J.P. Taylor, and the writer C. S. Lewis. Mr Conway and his fellow part-timers will have to battle hard to beat Magdalen's young bloods.

The Oxford team, average age just 23, have already chalked up the highest score in this series – 375 points – and hope to become the first college to win the title two years running.

[7] But win or lose, Birkbeck will have restored their reputation.

Mark Amado, Birkbeck's acting student union president, said: 'Last year's team suffered from stage fright. We trained harder this year because we wanted to show that Birkbeck is as good as – or even better than – other universities.'
Mail on Sunday

Why and how the structure works

[1] Starts with a very strong 'disaster' hook, reinforced with strong, emotional words such as 'laughing stock', 'slumping' and 'biggest defeat'. Introduces an amazing piece of information: Jeremy Paxman was sorry for them.

[2] Here's the 'Dear Reader' sentence which turns into the 'Dear Reader' par: what the feature is all about. Things have changed dramatically and 'the greatest challenge is yet to come'.

[3] The scene has been set and the curtain is about to go up on this drama. So first meet the college and the cast. This section describes the present situation, recalls the back history and reveals how the previous team was chosen.

[4] A second 'nub par' alerts the reader about the new selection and training process.

[5] Time to discover how they fared in the earlier rounds.

[6] This section contrasts the combatants: their differing history, location, alumni, liquidity . . .

[7] The end echoes the start but what a change of tone. This time the words and the message are positive. There's been a complete turnaround. The quote reinforces how proud Birkbeck people are.

Alas, Birkbeck lost – but won the praise and publicity stakes.

Three features

The features that follow are not flawlessly crafted exhibits from the Museum of the Written Word, reverently preserved under glass in subdued lighting. They're here because they work: the writing flows, the details are graphic and the words are well chosen.

National daily newspaper

ABBEY OVERFLOWS FOR COMPTON

Matthew Engel attends a service to celebrate the cricketer whose innings has left an indelible imprint.

He was not royalty (not as such). He was not a great statesman (his politics were a touch, well, simplistic). He was not a candidate for Poets' Corner (judging from his contributions to the *Sunday Express*). He was not holy.

And yet Westminster Abbey was filled to overflowing yesterday to mark the passing of Denis Compton. Two thousand people turned up; a thousand had their applications rejected, the abbey's biggest case of over-subscription for a memorial service since Richard Dimbleby died in 1966.

Dimbleby died at the height of his broadcasting fame. Compton died on April 23, aged 78. No one under 50 can even have any memory of seeing him do what he did best: play cricket sublimely, and with an air that the whole thing was the most ridiculous lark.

And you would have to be pushing 60 to remember his apotheosis, the summer of 1947. Exactly 50 years ago this week, when an Old Trafford Test was on, just as it will be tomorrow, Compton scored 115 for England against South Africa, an innings described by Wisden as 'delightful and impudent'.

That was just one of the 18 centuries he scored that extraordinary summer, when Britain at last began to feel the war was over. Compton was the embodiment of that feeling. And thus when the Dean of Westminster said that we had gathered to give thanks for the life of Denis Compton, it did not feel like a clergyman's phrase, but the literal truth. We were not just remembering someone who happened to be amazingly successful (the idea of a man good enough to play both football and cricket for England is now unthinkable), we were honouring someone who made an indelible imprint on the life of the nation.

Among the 2,000 were many you would have expected: dozens of retired cricketers, one former prime minister (no prizes) and all the showbizzy Taverner-types with whom Compton mixed so easily.

But there were hundreds of unknown folk, too, and some highly improbable ones – like Dennis Skinner who was on his way to the Commons, asked what the fuss was, and was ushered in as a special guest.

Skinner watched Compton play at Derby. 'I expect we were miles apart politically. But he was an adventurer, wasn't he? He took risks. He was everything that Boycott wasn't.'

The ceremony itself was fairly standard issue: I Vow To Thee My Country, Jerusalem and Pomp and Circumstance to finish, but all beautifully done. The chairman of Arsenal read Let us Now Praise Famous Men; E W Swanton, still thunderous at 90, read Cardus on Lord's.

The address was given by Compton's one-time Middlesex teammate and long-standing buddy, J J Warr, who delved briefly into the treasure chest of Compton-iana. These tales mostly rely on Compo's famously casual attitude to everything.

'In May 1967 he announced he was going to have an enormous party for his 50th birthday. His mother phoned him and said: "It's a good idea, Denis, but you're only 49." It was one of the few occasions when he was early for anything.'

One did half-expect Compo to wander in at any moment, late and full of apologies. It could have been the young daredevil of 1947 or the old man – knee and hips crocked – leaning on his stick. He had star quality throughout his life, which is what brought us to the abbey.

The decision to stage the Compton ceremony, made by the Dean, Wesley Carr, appears to be part of a trend towards populism in abbey memorial services. Brian Johnston, Les Dawson and Bobby Moore have recently received this very final British accolade. In contrast, politicians are now usually dealt with at St Margaret's, Westminster.

The honour would not have bothered Compo that much. As Warr said, his CBE was last seen hanging round the neck of his Old English sheepdog. But he would have loved the occasion, and the chance for a last drink with his very special chums. All 2,000 of them.
Guardian, 2 July 1997

This is rich writing, covering a news event and adding so much more in background colour and detail. At the end readers have the sense of having been at the service. They know the hymns, the readings, who spoke the eulogy. 'We were there,' says Engel.

Readers learn a great detail about Compton, his cricket (particular score on a particular date on a particular ground and the number of centuries scored in a particular year), his character and lifestyle, his sporting abilities, his friends and admirers – and also about Britain in 1947. Also, details of the most heavily subscribed memorial services at Westminster Abbey, names of recent celebrities honoured, the location for many politicians' memorial services, and on and on. Even two visual images of Compton young and old. And it's all wrapped up with a conclusion including an affectionate anecdote, the 1940-ish word 'chums' and a feeling of the Abbey packed with friends and admirers paying tribute to a remarkable man.

The structure is not the usual sequential approach, but proceeds at first by negatives, builds up his reputation using figures and a contrast with the Richard Dimbleby memorial service, describes his career, starts on the ceremony, describes those present including a quote from a surprise attender, gives more details of the ceremony, then covers the address, goes back to other services and ends with an anecdote and an affectionate wrap. And it all flows smoothly with the genesis of each par discernible in the previous one.

Weekly b2b periodical

PICNIC IN THE BEDROOM

James Thomas, 36, joined London's Dorset Square Hotel as general manager in November 1996. 'Bedroom picnics' are the latest innovation he has dreamt up in his quest to provide home-from-home service.

Two or three mornings a week, I wake up in the hotel. If I've worked late the night before, I might decide to forgo a battle with the Underground and grab a spare room. As well as being convenient, this gives me a chance to see how the hotel operates from a customer's point of view.

If I have stayed overnight, I'll enjoy the luxury of eggs and bacon – and I'll always taste the coffee and pastries to check the quality of our supplies.

⊘ If I've come in from home, I'll get in between 8 and 9am. The first thing I'll do is read the night manager's book and check up on the overnight occupancy and room rates.

My morning will be spent around reception, chatting to guests, opening mail and speaking to maintenance and housekeeping. This is a small hotel – only 38 bedrooms – so my job as general manager is very much hands-on. We're all multi-faceted here. For instance, we don't have a personnel or training manager, so my job encompasses both those roles.

⊘ Every Tuesday morning at 11am, I meet with the other hotel general managers in the Firmdale group at the company's head office in South Kensington. There are just five of us, all managing small luxury hotels in London. The others are women, which is great because they're so chatty. I know that's a sexist thing to say, but I have to be sexist because I'm the underdog.

At lunchtime I'll spend some time in the kitchen watching the service. I'll then nip out for a sandwich from the deli on the corner. I could get something to eat in the hotel but it's important to get off the premises just for 20 minutes, especially if I've stayed in the hotel the previous night.

It's also necessary to observe what's going on in the local area. For instance, by going out of the hotel, we discovered that many of our US guests were skipping breakfast in the hotel and grabbing a bagel from the deli before jumping into a taxi en route to their meetings. So we've now introduced 'Breakfast to go'. Five minutes after ordering it, guests can pick up a Dorset Square Hotel paper bag – containing juice, coffee and a pastry – from reception as they go out the door.

⊘ About 2.30pm I disappear into my broom cupboard of an office to get on with some paperwork. This is also a chance to develop new ideas. It's important to be creative. You can't afford to stand still – it's good for business and it stops the staff getting bored.

My latest project is 'Bedroom picnics', a name that we're going to trademark. The idea stems from last summer, when I returned from the theatre one night with a girlfriend and we felt a bit peckish, but weren't sure what we wanted to eat. Our head chef, Trevor Baines, said he would put together a few nibbly bits. It was great – a selection of all the kinds of things you like to eat in a relaxed way.

We've now developed the idea for room service. It is served on a large wicker tray with a green gingham cloth – perfect for putting on the bed to eat while watching the television, planning your next day's meeting, running the bath – or even in the bath. We wanted to get away from formal room service and provide something that guests can pick at with their fingers in the relaxed setting of their room.

The contents must be simple enough to be put together in a few minutes, even by the night porter. A typical picnic would include vegetable crudités and a dip, a selection of cold meat such as salami, Parma ham and turkey, hot Toulouse sausages with an onion and mustard dip, prawns in filo pastry, smoked salmon, cheese, bread and freshly sliced fruit.

I am just as likely to deliver the Bedroom picnic to a guest's room myself as is one of the restaurant staff.

⊕ At about 6pm I write personal arrival notes to all the guests, which are delivered at turn-down. We know every guest's name and what kind of business they're in. Every Thursday evening between 6 and 7pm, all guests are invited for cocktails in the restaurant.

⊘ I'll eat dinner in the hotel restaurant – the Potting Shed – two or three times a week. If not, I leave the hotel between 8 and 9pm. By then most of the arrivals are in, the turn-downs are done and the restaurant is buzzing. Going home to Docklands is a great antidote to all this – I read or watch TV.

Janet Harmer, *Caterer and Hotelkeeper*, 11 June 1998

Reproduced with the permission of the editor of *Caterer and Hotelkeeper*.

The feature was accompanied by a Factfile on the hotel, including address, telephone numbers, owner, number of bedrooms and room rates.

This is a variation on the *Sunday Times* 'Life in the Day of' page. The feature profiles a catering personality by describing a typical working day which exemplifies many. It includes a great deal of valuable hotel information: staffing attitudes, how often figures are checked, managers' meetings, how ideas to generate extra breakfast income are developed, a new idea – copiable under a different name – and how to run it, guest pampering, etc. The writing is deceptively simple, mostly in the present tense and requires no links except the use of the time. The style fits the catering and hotel business: hard-working, gossipy, people-oriented and rather like show business with its search for the new. By the end, the reader has a very good idea of the hotel and its general manager, together with some new ideas to ponder and maybe adapt.

Glossy monthly magazine

I LOVE THE JOB, BUT DO I HAVE TO WEAR THAT HAT?

Uniforms have come a long way since the nylon overall – or have they? Getting your corporate kit on can provoke mixed feelings, as Kerry Fowler discovers.

There's something about a woman in uniform, whether she's selling a low-rate mortgage or serving a G&T at 30,000 feet. When they're right, the clothes inspire confidence: trust me, they say. When they're wrong, the company looks tacky and the trendiest woman feels frumpy, no matter how hard she tries. As Leonie Barrie, Editor of *Company Clothing* magazine (the industry's style bible), says, 'It's a very emotive subject. People who have to wear uniforms are acutely aware of others' reactions.'

Uniforms flash up all sorts of message – fear (ticket collectors and traffic wardens), respect (look how far Deirdre's 'airline pilot' in *Coronation Street* fell from grace when it turned out he was just a silk-tie hawker) and instant recognition of who's staff and who isn't ('Ask the man in the hat, he'll know'). 'A uniform signals competence, kindliness and a host of other skills much more dramatically than the way you sit or stand, or the expression on your face,' says Halla Beloff, social psychologist at Edinburgh University.

Granted, if you have to wear a Mrs Overall pinny your expression may not have the same radiance as the girl at the Dior counter, but at least these practical numbers keep clothes clean. Better still, they simplify life. GH nutritionist Fiona Hunter is wistful about the white cotton dress she wore as a hospital dietician. 'I had 15 minutes extra in bed,' she says. 'I didn't have to think about what to wear. I didn't have to spend money on work clothes and it was all laundered for me. Now I have a clothes crisis every morning.'

But isn't that preferable to getting kitted up to look like Nell Gwynne? Not according to the supervisor at the Beefeater By the Tower (of London) restaurant. 'Dressing up is all part of the job,' she says. 'Sometimes the girls don't like the mob caps, but otherwise they enjoy it.' And what of the message conveyed by their wench-type costumes? Surprisingly, she's never had a problem in all her 23 years there. 'The outfits are quite demure and the maids have to wear discreet white bras under the camisole. We do get the occasional enquiry as to whether we're a topless restaurant but, that aside, we don't really tend to get rude comments,' she says.

Confusion is much more likely at London's trendy Pharmacy restaurant (part-owned by Damien Hirst), where the receptionists wear Prada-designed doctors' coats and the waiters have surgeons' jackets. Are they there to give you a good time or serve up a prognosis you wonder.

No such mystery surrounds the tartan army at Caledonian Airways, who thrive on the attention their kilts and frilly jabots bring. 'Americans are wild about them,' says purser Jill Mellor. 'We get stopped on concourses all round the world by people wanting to know who we work for.' A hefty staff manual details everything from the position of the kilt pin to the tilt of the tam o' shanter.

'The quality of the outfit shows workers the kind of respect paid by the employer,' says Halla Beloff. 'What they wear has to inspire confidence. It has to be clean and decent, but it should also be up to date and it certainly shouldn't be bizarre. A bad uniform can put you in a bad mood and you need to feel good if you're interacting with people.'

Elizabeth, now a dance teacher, is still spooked by her experience in a Sainsbury's uniform 10 years ago. 'I can't express how much I hated wearing it,' she says. 'I looked like a bell – a big orange and brown nylon bell. But,' she adds, 'I did meet my husband while I was on the checkout . . .'

These days, many companies turn to fashion designers for help.

Sainsbury's has signed up Paul Costelloe, who revamped BA; John Rocha designs for Virgin Airlines; Bruce Oldfield has put together a range of workwear for everyone from nurses to chefs; and Jeff Banks has left his mark on Asda, Barclays Bank, Iceland and many more. 'It's a major status symbol,' says Jeff. 'Organisations spend a lot on graphics and literature and finally the penny drops: if you want to make a company buzz, make sure the staff are happy with the way they look.' Designers can't afford any catwalk preciousness, though. 'They're not just catering for size 8–18s, it's more like 6–40s,' says Leonie Barrie. 'They've also got to think about ethnic designs and maternity wear.'

So what's the secret of creating a classy livery? 'There's a reason why I say wardrobe and not uniform,' says Jeff, who estimates around 500,000 people spend the day in his corporate designs. 'The wardrobe I did for Barclays has a printed "flippy" skirt and shaped blouse that would suit an 18-year-old and a looser over-shirt, pleated skirt and loose striped jacket that would be fine for a 55-year-old woman. (If you're over 50 and still feeling flippy, the choice of skirts is up to you.) But they still look as if they play for the same team.'

You can be a team-player even if you're not in front of house, and most occupations have an unwritten dress code – pin-stripes for accountants, chinos for computer buffs, Armani for media moguls.

Sometimes it's more prescriptive: at John Lewis, while the 'partners' (as the rank and file are known) wear navy and green outfits, the section managers select from Jaeger or Country Casuals, and choose from black and blue, too. It's like the old sixth-form privilege: instead of a boater you get to wear a skull cap.

London barrister Barbara Hewson conforms to a dress code devised over 200 years ago: 'Nothing much has changed except the price – the horsehair wig now costs around £340.' For fledgling legal eagles, though, it can be worth the outlay. 'Your client immediately knows who you are when you're in your kit,' she says.

The perverse psychology is that none of us wants to be a clone. Schoolgirls aren't the only ones to customise their uniforms. The Britannia stewardesses in the TV documentary *Airline* are asked to wear red lipstick to match their corporate scarf but, apparently, some slide down the spectrum until they hit pink. We all, it seems, like to be unique beneath the serge.
Good Housekeeping, June 1998

A lot of research went into this feature – 19 firms or types of business are mentioned and seven people are quoted – yet the whole flows smoothly. The writing is full of images, which is as it should be since the subject is visual. The lively quotes give insight into the subject.

The range of uniforms covered is impressively wide: from airlines to supermarkets, theme restaurants to posh eateries, barristers to schoolgirls. The quotes read well and are in different voices, suggesting that the writer can probably do shorthand and doesn't recast everything into her own style.

There's a deft touch with words: 'radiance' is used as a semi-sendup for a girl at the Dior counter, contrasting with 'tacky' and 'frumpy' elsewhere; the nutritionist is 'wistful' about the pluses of her old uniformed life. There's evidence of practical thinking and questioning: the sizes that are catered for, for example, and different styles for different age and size groups.

The piece runs smoothly because of deft linking and by the end the reader has been entertained, informed and enlightened.

4
Writing columns and blogs

This is a very short chapter, by far the shortest in the book, not because there is little to say on the subject but because the chapters on feature writing, writing online and style cover the important points and there is no need to repeat them here. However, there are one or two things to emphasise.

The general advice on how to write good features copy applies with particular force to columns and blogs[1]. The more you expect the reader to choose your piece rather than the one next to it or after it – on the grounds that it's more interesting to read – the more you need a distinctive style and the harder you may have to work to achieve it.

While there are obvious differences between the two forms, there are also differences between what could be called public opinionated writing – on politics, sport, crime – and personal confessional writing on sex, disease (particularly if it's terminal) and, yes, crime again. So a blog by a politician, political journalist or activist will be less emotionally revealing than a printed column on 'the cancer that's killing me' or 'my fun times as an escort'.

What is distinctive and important about blogging is that, at least in principle, anybody can do it. There is no need to follow a course, pass a test or persuade the editor to print what you write.

It remains to be seen whether – and to what extent – blogging will replace column writing. When Eric Zorn, a columnist and blogger on the *Chicago Tribune*, compared the two forms in 2007[2] he put forward six arguments in favour of blogging, eg that it offers immediate access to readers, is highly

---

1   See also Chapter 6, 'Writing for digital publication – shortform', page 128.
2   Available online at http://bit.ly/zorncolumn (accessed 23 November 2015).

interactive and has no fixed length. Of his three arguments in favour of column writing, one of them – it brings more readers, more impact and more money – obviously trumps all the others. But as he pointed out, this wouldn't necessarily remain true for all time . . .

Columnists on columns

Include lots of facts, preferably things readers are unlikely to know; choose a subject that can be expressed in a single phrase; refine any argument until it is clear in your head; the opening needs to work immediately: it should affront readers, or make them laugh, or puzzle them in an engaging way; the columnist who does no original work is a dud.
Andrew Marr, *My Trade*

There must not be too many ideas (two or three will usually suffice), but plenty of opinions; the bland, obvious or fence-sitting must be ruthlessly expunged. Columns are there to get a reaction – agreement, disagreement, amusement, enlightenment. Intolerance is often a virtue. 'So what?' will not do. The column must sustain its theme, building towards a climax or pay-off line. If it wanders the reader will wander on.
Peter Cole, *Guardian*

Stamina is most important, as is unflagging curiosity touched with passion.
Stephen Glover of the *Daily Mail* in *Press Gazette*

Don't get disheartened when you receive the inevitable hate mail that being a really good columnist brings. If you've made someone seethe, then you've made them think and that's your job. . . . Besides, the vitriolic ones make good firelighters, I find.
Stacia Briggs of the *Evening News*, Norwich, in *Press Gazette*

What most columnists don't get is that we are part of the entertainment industry as well. You know, there's no divine right to be read and I like to think that people who turn to my page don't know if they're going to get a polemic or a song and dance act or a page of jokes.
Richard Littlejohn of the *Daily Mail*, in *British Journalism Review*

If you can make the readers laugh or just smile you've probably got their attention, no matter what the subject matter. But don't force it, never, never force it. Facetiousness is not attractive. . . . Writing a funny column can be the most difficult labour of all. But when it works it's also the most satisfying.
Barry Norman of *Radio Times*

Sometimes, just sometimes, columns are easy. An idea or story captures your imagination, an arresting opening line presents itself, and the piece flows from your fingers as they skip joyfully and unstoppably across the keyboard. It makes perfect sense, it has the right pace and rhythm, it's funny, it hits a nerve and everyone writes in to say they laughed and/or agreed with you.

This happens about once every five years. For the remaining 209 weeks you must fake it. You must fake it like a ballerina fakes smiling, up on her bleeding, battered toes, by writing and rewriting, striking out dud phrases and bringing in new ones that turn out to be even worse and abandoning them without a backward glance too. It's awful.
Lucy Mangan of the *Guardian*

Any good column has three ingredients: (1) a figure from an obscure source (quoted in brackets); (2) a reference to a current film; (3) a list; and (4) an arrogant disregard for the rules of maths. And grammar. With a mix of short and long sentences. For dramatic effect.

As for inspiration I scour daily newspapers and cut out any bizarre stories, particularly from overseas. I keep the cuts somewhere under the pile of old newspapers on top of my desk. This eases the panic over having nothing to write about when 40 minutes from deadline.

I can't ever find the cuts but knowing they're there somehow helps. And having an untidy desk makes me look busy and intellectual.

Finally, always write to length . . .
Martin Freeman of the *Evening Herald*, Plymouth, in *Press Gazette*

He didn't write to length – and he went on to complain (tongue-in-cheek) about the subs who would therefore have to cut his copy. Had he been blogging, of course, he and they wouldn't have had that problem.

5
Writing reviews

Harriett Gilbert

What is a review?

You are already a reviewer. Every time you explain to a friend why such and such a movie doesn't work, or describe the excellence of so and so's new album, you are in effect reviewing an art work or an entertainment: in other words, you are providing a critical assessment of it. That is what a review does.

A 'listing' is different. It need do nothing more than provide the reader or listener with factual information:

> 9.00 Russell Howard's Good News: Stand-up comedy

A review, as well as providing that kind of information, should describe the work and express an opinion about it.

What does it take to be a reviewer?

This raises a fundamental question. Although everyone has a right to express their opinion, why should certain opinions have the privilege of being published? Why should a small group of journalists be allowed to discourage strangers from buying a book they might otherwise have read, or urge them to spend their money on expensive concert tickets?

The internet, in its democratic way, may allow anyone and everyone to publish reviews of books, films, hotels and so on – and we shall return to this later – but professional, paid reviewers, whether online or in print, do indeed form a privileged elite.

One justification is that they perform a service. With so much art and entertainment to choose from, critical sifting is vital. Another is that a good reviewer accepts that the privilege of influencing strangers carries responsibilities.

The first is to know what you are talking about. You should, at least, have seen, eaten at, listened to or read the thing you are reviewing. It is not enough (as occasionally happens) to rewrite or even copy a publicist's blurb.

You should also know what you like, what you hate and why. If, for instance, you find that all television programmes are trivial and uninteresting, think again before pursuing a career as a television critic. This does not mean that your tastes should be set in cement (indeed, it would be extremely odd if they stayed the same throughout your life); it simply means you should care.

There are some who argue that, more than that, you should be an expert in your field. There is much to be said for expertise – and, if you want to make reviewing the central plank of your career, you should undoubtedly work to acquire expertise in your chosen area – but a useful review may still be written by a thoughtful beginner or occasional reviewer.

In fact, a beginner or occasional reviewer can sometimes have the edge. As A A Gill has said about his job as a restaurant critic:

> In most jobs experience is a boon, but for a critic it puts an ever-lengthening distance between you and your reader. The vast majority of diners don't eat with knowledge, they eat with friends. They don't know what happens on the other side of the swing door. Why should they? Most people eat out rarely and with high expectations, not every day with a knowing smirk.

All reviewers should be aware that experience and knowledge remove them from their readers. For instance, because they experience so much that is bad – stuff from which they protect the public with their subsequent panning reviews – they should recognise that sometimes, in gratitude, they see the merely good as being brilliant. And their physical encounter with the things they review is rarely the same as the punters'. On the one hand, they usually have the best theatre seats, and can visit art shows before the public surges in to obscure the exhibits. Often, too, they receive advance tapes of television and radio programmes to watch or listen to whenever convenient. On the other hand, they may be summoned to *group* television previews, in preview theatres not obviously designed to resemble comfortable sitting rooms; and critics usually watch films in the morning, in cinemas empty except for them and a taciturn scattering of their colleagues. A good reviewer should bear these abnormalities in mind.

Some artists find it objectionable for their work to be reviewed by non-practitioners. Book critics are, at least, writers. Some of them have even written books. But many reviewers of film, theatre, art, dance, music and so on have never actually practised the form, however great their theoretical knowledge.

Painters frequently complain about their work being judged by 'art historians' (the way they spit out those two words would lead you to suppose they were talking about kitten torturers). Theatre people are even more vociferous – for two reasons.

The first is purely economic. Every performance of a play is expensive, what with wages, lighting, rental of the theatre and so on. So, if the first-night reviews are hostile, companies cannot afford to continue performing to empty or half-empty houses, hoping that audiences will gradually be drawn by word of mouth. The second reason is that theatre is *immediate*. Film-makers, writers and painters, in contrast, have long ago finished creating their work by the time the reviews appear. And, although of course they suffer whenever their work is damned, the process is even more painful for those who must read of their failures and inadequacies when, in effect, they are still in the process of creating.

And drama critics can have an extraordinary influence. So great was the power of the New York critic Clive Barnes that Broadway managements are said to have scoured the telephone directories for other Clive Barneses, invited them along to opening nights and pasted their praise – 'The best play I've seen: Clive Barnes' – on the flanks of their theatres.

But still: does this mean that reviewers should also be practitioners? Many in the British theatre think so and, in order to prove their point, they once challenged the drama critics to try directing a play. A few accepted, including the notoriously scathing Nicholas de Jongh of the London *Evening Standard*. The resultant productions were widely agreed to be worthy at best, terrible at worst. While this may have gratified the challengers, however, it proved only that good reviewers are *not* necessarily good practitioners.

It is important to understand the limitations and potential of an art form – to recognise, for instance, that a play can do things that a film cannot, and vice versa – but it is not essential to be able to practise it yourself.

If the anger of theatre people is caused, in part, by the devastating power of bad reviews, it is also caused by a widespread belief (among artists) that the primary role of reviewers is to nurture and promote the form about which they write.

It certainly is an important role. Obscure bands; avant-garde artists; authors attempting new forms of fiction: without the encouragement and publicity pro-vided by sympathetic reviewers, these would have an even harder time than they do gaining recognition. Art critics such as *Time Out*'s Sarah Kent helped to promote and explain the New British Artists. Or, slightly different example: years before video games were taken seriously enough to win Bafta awards, Rhianna Pratchett, now herself a leading game writer, was reviewing and thoughtfully analysing games in *PC Zone*. The marginalised, new or difficult rely on critics to promote, explain and support them.

Well-established, commercial art forms are also helped by intelligent reviewing. Film critics such as Dilys Powell and Judith Williamson, for instance, have given their readers a deeper appreciation of popular cinema. But if critics did *nothing* but support and praise – or, indeed, nothing but carp and condemn – they would cease to have any impact. Their work would lose credibility and focus.

A paradox to be borne in mind is that readers frequently take their bearings from regular critics with whom they disagree but of whose preferences they are aware. If they know that a critic routinely dismisses or disparages something they enjoy, readers are perfectly capable of taking a thumbs-down as a thumbs-up. The clearer your views, the better you enable them to do this.

Write for your reader

Centrally, critics must write for their readers, not for the artists whose work they are assessing (nor for fellow reviewers, however much they would like their good opinion). This does not mean that critics' opinions should twist and turn to make their readers happy; it means that critics should serve their readers. To do this, they must know who their readers are.

The readers of redtop tabloids, for instance, expect very few reviews – mainly previews of television programmes – but, what they get, they like to be short and snappy, followed as a rule by a 'star rating' (five stars for 'Don't miss it', one for 'Garbage', to quote the *Daily Star*). At the other end of the newspaper market, although space for arts coverage is shrinking, readers still appreciate longer, more carefully argued reviews. A lead book review in the *Observer*, for example, might run to 1,000 words of description, argument and opinion. (Occasionally, reviews in the broadsheets never get to the opinion bit at all, especially reviews of biographies by writers who were acquainted with the subject and choose to devote their space to reminiscence. This is not an example to be followed.)

There are magazines – from GQ to the *New Statesman* – that also run single reviews of 1,000 words or more. But most, even among the glossy monthlies, do not. This is partly because their designers refuse to have pages packed with grey columns of words. It is also because, when they do choose to run a lengthy piece on the arts, it is more likely to be in the form of a feature. So *Red* might run an interview of over 1,500 words with the actress Natalie Portman but, in the same issue, have a lead film review (of *Suite Française*) that's scarcely 350 words long, with subsidiary reviews of under 50 words each. Even *Time Out*, a magazine of which reviews are an important component, usually runs them at between 250 and 400 words, no more.

The time your readers expect to devote to reading your review is important, but length is far from being everything. Tone of voice and cultural references matter too. See how Jon Ronson's book about 'social media fury', *So You've Been Publicly Shamed*, is reviewed in two very different publications. *Red* is a women's lifestyle magazine primarily concerned with fashion, beauty, relationships and celebrities. Its review of the book begins like this:

> Jon Ronson is one of the funniest writers we have, as George Clooney will tell you (he bought the rights to Ronson's book *The Men Who Stare At Goats* and then starred in the film).

And that celebrity heart-throb endorsement makes up more than half of the 50-word review. In the *Guardian* the same book is given in the region of 2,000 words and, although the review also refers to *The Men Who Stare At Goats*, it doesn't mention George Clooney. Instead, it mentions the 'Bilderberg Group' as though its readers will know, or be flattered by the assumption that they know, what the organisation is.

Similarly, when writing for the now defunct feminist magazine *Sibyl*, the literary critic Georgina Paul could talk of the 'feminist reappropriation' of ancient Greek myth; her readers would have understood what she meant. Had she been writing for a local paper, the phrase would have needed to be explained or (preferably) replaced.

Readers of local papers are perhaps the hardest to target. You know where they live, and should take that into account when reviewing things connected to the area, but, even more than with national papers, they tend to differ widely in age, income, education, cultural interests and politics. At least with most of the national press you know your readers' probable politics and incomes.

Magazines are more narrowly focused. They may, overtly or otherwise, be aimed at a particular sex or age group. There are magazines for people with such and such a hobby, job, cultural interest, religion, political affiliation. There are even magazines aimed at people of a particular ethnic group or sexual orientation.

Their readers, of course, usually buy a whole range of publications. To take just one example: a black British woman estate agent might regularly read *Estates Gazette*, the *Daily Mail*, *Cosmopolitan* and *Pride*. Only in *Pride*, a magazine specifically aimed at black readers, would she expect a review of a gig by the Senegalese musician Cheikh Lo to open as Diana Evans's did:

The Jazz Café is brimming with swaying 'world music' fans, most of whom, it has to be said, are white. It's the same with most concerts by African stars. The question arises, why is it that black people don't listen to their own music?

Whether your publication's readers are black people, schoolteachers, film buffs, train spotters, gays, vegetarians, pensioners or clubbers, your review should recognise that fact.

Once you have established who your readers are – their likely interests, frame of reference, verbal attention span and so on – there are five further questions which, if you are to serve them well, you should ask yourself:

- Have I given the thing I'm reviewing my full, open-minded attention?
- Have I reached my assessment of it honestly: uninfluenced, for instance, by the fear of being out on a limb, the fear of upsetting the powerful, the temptation to be nasty for the fun of it or the simple pleasure of kicking someone when they're up?
- Have I made my assessment clear?
- Have I provided my readers with enough descriptive and factual information for them to decide the value of my assessment?
- Is what I've written engaging – *to my particular readers?*

THE SCARE: *Chivalry.* This is the battle for The Scare's soul: righteous, inventive punk-rock versus gin-soaked rock'n'roll outlaw spirit with a one-way ticket to severe traction. From the moment 'Bats! Bats! Bats!' rolls in on a growling disco-rock bassline, we're met with the soundtrack to Iggy's own swingers party and it's stirring stuff. A good deal of its success is to do with the way Wade Keighran grinds the basslines like scars into the flesh of the songs, creating a pool of blood for singer Kiss Reid to writhe around in – himself some deranged hybrid of Mick Jagger and *Teen Wolf.* But *Chivalry* is about more than just cheap thrills. 'Eighty Eight' hides its fangs behind a rolling surf-pop lick and 'Swamp' sounds exactly like a song called 'Swamp' is supposed to. Order? Chaos? Who cares? In appropriating the most dangerous bits of everything The Scare have whipped up a fright to remember.
NME

BULLY BEEF AND BURGHERS by James Callaway (published by the author at 54 Swain Street, Watchet, Somerset TA23). Railway preservationists may recall the author as a volunteer stationmaster at Abergynolwyn, on the Talyllyn Railway; he has now transferred to the broad gauge and is a supporter of the West Somerset Railway. This, his second book, is set on the British army-controlled railways of South Africa during the Boer War and concerns the military and amorous activities of Captain Robin Goodfellow, Royal Engineers, and his misadventures with an armoured train nicknamed 'Bully Beef'. It is a good-natured romp and greatly assisted your reviewer to survive a tedious train journey.
Railway Magazine

How to research

The amount of research you need do depends on three things. First is the ambitiousness of your review. A 1,000-word review of *Lolita* in which you intend to discuss the general issue of movie censorship will obviously need more preparatory reading than a straightforward 200-word review.

Second is the amount of information available. To review a Patti Smith concert, for instance, you would need to become familiar not only with decades' worth of her work but with the accumulation of comment about it. The same would not be true for a concert by a new performer.

Third, and in practice most important, is the amount of time you have. Specialist reviewers never stop researching, if only because their present work is a form of research for the future. Occasional reviewers must do what they can within the restraints of the deadline. And, although it is impossible to know too much, it is worth remembering that knowledge works best as a quiet foundation for what you write, not as rococo decoration splattered about all over the place. Its purpose is not to impress the readers with your brilliance, but to ensure the solidity and soundness of your judgment.

The most important element in research is examples of previous work (if any) by the artist or entertainer in question. These allow you to spot recurrent themes, obsessions, strengths and weaknesses and to assess the relationship of the new work to the old.

The internet, too, is obviously invaluable, although do remember to double-check everything you read there. For example, while an artist's own site is likely to have up-to-date information about tour dates, publications, film roles or whatever, it is most unlikely to contain information detrimental to the artist's reputation. Similarly, although Wikipedia is a go-to site for all kinds of information, its entries vary widely in terms of accuracy, detail and currency.

If you want to become a specialist reviewer, you might subscribe to an authoritative online service such as Oxford Reference (www.oxfordreference. com/) or Oxford Music Online (www.oxfordmusiconline.com/public/), which includes the magisterial Grove Music Online. Or you might prefer to buy, or borrow, reference books, in which case those that reviewers have found useful include *The Penguin Dictionary of Art and Artists*, *The Penguin Encyclopedia of Popular Music*, *The Macmillan International Film Encyclopedia*, *Time Out Film Guide* and indeed many of the Oxford University Press reference works in book form.

Take the right notes

In most cases, you will have one chance to watch or listen to the work you are reviewing. Even with CDs, DVDs and books, although in theory you can return to the beginning as often as you like, in practice there may not be time for more than one go. So try to ensure that the notes you take are the right ones.

You need, first, to note those *facts* that you will need when you start to write: that the novel's narrator is a 60-year-old lawyer, for example; or that the opera has been relocated to 1930s Berlin.

Sense impressions are also important: the look of a stage set; the way the actor playing Hamlet uses his voice; the lighting of a rock concert; the dominant colours of a movie . . . whatever strikes you, make sufficient notes to be able to recreate it in print. And do keep *all* your senses alert. A film, for instance, is more than its narrative. It is also a complex of composition, lighting, movement and noise. As well as dialogue, the sound track will almost certainly have music on it, not to mention the sighing of wind or the constant throbbing of helicopter blades. The camera may cling to the actors' faces in close-up, or keep its distance.

Similarly, a dance performance consists not only of a sequence of movements more or less effectively performed, but also of music (or other sounds), lighting, costume and decor. Notice, *consciously* notice, all those things that are having an effect.

Quotes, where applicable, are also useful. Write down those that are powerful in themselves and those that could be used to make a wider point.

Finally, note your reactions. If you smile, choke up, are frightened, are bored, put it down.

After all this, the next point to make is that you can take *too many* notes. Especially when reviewing a performance, if you spend all your time with your face in a notebook you are liable to miss key moments. So, be selective: note only those things that make a special impression.

Some critics make no notes at all until a performance is over, on the not unreasonable grounds that what they remember must be what most impressed them. If you trust your memory, try it. And, even if you have cautiously taken notes during the performance, it is still useful to write a quick sentence afterwards, to sum up your feelings: 'Pretentious rubbish; I couldn't understand a word of it', for instance, or 'Started slowly but, by the end, had me gripped.' The reason for this is to prevent you, later, from writing yourself towards an untruthful opinion. For various reasons, including doubts about your judgment, this is easy to do.

Structure

As with any piece of journalism, you cannot decide on the structure of a review until you know what the story is – or more precisely, in the case of a review, whether you plan to give the work a thumbs-up, a thumbs-down or something in between. You also need to know why you have reached your verdict.

Take, for instance, this short review of Simple Minds' *Néapolis* album (published in the *Big Issue*):

> Once masters of stomping stadium rock, the Minds have become a watered-down version of atmospheric U2 pop circa the 'Zooropa' LP. Although there are charming touches such as 'War Babies', the likes of recent single 'Glitterball' will soon have you dozing off. Things improve with 'Androgyny', but when they finished recording the album in crime-ridden Naples (hence its title) any decent melodies they had must have been mugged and left for dead.

The reviewer, Gary Crossing, is giving the album a thumbs-down because, he believes, it demonstrates how musically *boring* Simple Minds have become. The structure of his review depends on this assessment. First, because he has few words to play with, he has ignored those aspects of the album irrelevant to his central point. This does not mean that he has suppressed the album's virtues – merely that he has put to one side those ingredients he considers peripheral: here, for example, the musicians' technical ability.

Second, to show the extent of his disappointment, he opens by reminding his readers that the band were once 'masters of stomping stadium rock'.

Then, what little praise he has to offer is sandwiched in the middle of the piece, the place where it has the least impact. The opening and closing sentences talk of 'watered-down' and 'left for dead'.

Crucial to the structure of reviews is the way in which you arrange your blocks of positive and negative comment. The worst solution, because it leaves your readers feeling dizzy, is to zigzag from one to the other throughout the review: 'This is great, but on the other hand, but then again, but then again . . .' It is clearer to have substantial blocks of points in favour and points against.

For instance, if you are reviewing a novel, it is best to avoid slaloming your way around every single aspect of the book – plot, characters, style, form, message and so on – allocating plus and minus points to each. Instead, you should first put aside the least significant or interesting aspects, then, with what you have left, create solid building blocks of praise and condemnation, regardless of the aspect being praised or condemned. Thus you might, in one block, praise a novel for its prose style, intelligence and humour and, in another, criticise its political insensitivity, for instance.

How you arrange these, however, can vary. Reviewing a book you enjoyed a lot, you might decide to open with praise, have a small block of negative comment in the middle, then finish with another substantial block of praise. Or you might decide to open with what you think is wrong with it (but expressing it in such a way that your readers can guess a 'but' is coming), then move into a substantial block of praise that continues to the end. Or, if what you dislike is trivial, you could position the negative comment as a fleeting parenthesis at the end: 'The novel may lack the full-throttle pace and finely tuned plotting of its predecessor, but the raucous humour is still firing on all cylinders.'

You will also need to decide where to place the basic factual information: to tell the reader precisely what it *is* that's being reviewed. Depending on the convention of your newspaper or magazine, there will be a format for putting some of this, as a matter of course, before the start of the review. The movie magazine *Empire*, for instance, precedes each review with the following: film title; release date; certification; director; main actors; a snappy summary of the plot. Less expansively, a *Sunday Times* book review opens with the title of the work, the author, the publisher, the price and the number of pages; no plot summary. So: '*Déjà Dead* by Kathy Reichs Heinemann £10 pp 416' – which tells the reader something, but not enough. Is this a work of non-fiction or fiction? If the latter, what *kind* of fiction? A novel or stories? What's the genre? What's the book about? Especially because this was Kathy Reichs's debut, the reviewer needed to answer all this pretty quickly.

This need not necessarily mean in the opening sentence or paragraph (see 'Intros', below) but certainly before proceeding with any kind of detailed criticism.

Extra thought is needed if you are writing a round-up review: of the highlights from last night's television, the month's new movies, the best in recent science fiction or whatever. For this, you will need to consider how to make the elements work together, including the order in which they should be placed.

Where order is concerned, there are two straightforward solutions. You could either start with the programme, film or novel you liked most, allocating it the greatest share of words, and proceed downwards (in liking and word-length) from there. Or you could start with the most newsworthy, the one of which most of your readers will have heard, the one by the most famous artist, and, again, work downwards from there.

But these are not the only options. To take just one example: you might choose to allocate the greatest share of words to the programme, film or novel you most hated. If that seems appropriate, do it.

The other question is how to link the disparate elements of the review. If an overall theme suggests itself, pick it up and run with it. If, however, the works have little in common, then rather than try to crush them into a framework in which they are uncomfortable you might prefer to use some kind of link to attach one review to the next. For instance, in a round-up review of movies in the *Observer*, Philip French finds a link like this. First, he ends his review of a heist thriller called *The Lookout*:

> As with *Fargo*, the snow is thick on the ground and ends up soaked with blood. It's a competent film, and Jeff Daniels is, as always, first rate as the hero's blind flatmate.

Then he moves to his next review:

> There is even more blood and far more snow in *30 Days of Night*, a horror movie set in northern Alaska, starring Danny Huston as the leader of a pack of carnivorous vampires speaking some Transylvanian dialect.

If there are neither obvious links nor any obvious common theme, it is usually best not to push it. Simply type a full stop after one review, breathe, then proceed to the next.

Past or present tense?

Before you start writing, there is one small grammatical question to consider. Should you use the past tense or the present? The rule is more or less simple. Events that will have come and gone by the time the review is published – one-off concerts, for instance, or television or radio programmes – are usually described in the past tense:

> As adroitly as a snake charmer coaxing a sleepy cobra from its basket, he *persuaded* 98-year-old Frances Partridge, the last of the Bloomsbury group, to talk about her marriage. [My italics]
> Sue Arnold reviewing a programme in Michael Berkeley's Radio 3 series
> *Private Passions* in the *Observer*

The past tense could also be appropriate to describe an event at which something took place that will probably not be repeated: a performance of a play in which an understudy took over to rapturous applause, for instance.

Otherwise, the convention is to use the present tense:

> It's 1970 and the streets are thick with chaos during a state of emergency declared by General Franco's right-wing regime. En route to hospital, a prostitute *gives* birth on a bus . . . [My italics]
> Martin Aston reviewing Pedro Almodóvar's movie *Live Flesh* in *Neon*

Intros

As with features, there are no rules about how a review should open – except that, as with all journalism, the words should snatch the reader's attention and be relevant, directly or obliquely, to the main point you intend to make. There are, however, a number of tried and tested formulas.

The most straightforward is to step straight in with the basic factual information referred to in 'Structure' above. Thus John Dugdale, reviewing a batch of crime novels in the *Sunday Times*, opens like this:

> Set in the winter of 1586–7, Patricia Finney's *Unicorn's Blood* asks why the Virgin Queen eventually succumbed to her advisers' pressure to execute Mary, Queen of Scots, and hypothesises that spymaster Walsingham blackmailed her after acquiring a confessional youthful journal.

This approach could be deadly dull. A careless (or maybe distracted) sub once changed a reviewer's opening sentence from 'This is an historical novel about historical novels' to the rather less provocative and interesting 'This is an historical novel.' But starting with the basic information works when it is unusual or arresting: in John Dugdale's case, first because thrillers are not often set in the sixteenth century; second because of the widespread fascination with Mary, Queen of Scots. Describing Walsingham as a 'spymaster' also attracts attention. Calling him 'secretary of state', although no less truthful, would be less arresting.

In the same column, Dugdale reviews the Kathy Reichs novel referred to in 'Structure' above. Here, although again he opens with the basic, factual information, he gives it a critical twist.

> Kathy Reichs's *Déjà Dead* is so undisguisedly a DIY Patricia Cornwell novel that part of the considerable enjoyment of reading it lies in ticking off the formulaic features.

Crime-fiction fans will immediately know what a Patricia Cornwell novel is: will know that her regular heroine is a feisty forensic scientist who time and again solves gruesome murders before the mystified police can. Assuming that most of his readers will be fans, Dugdale has therefore taken the risk of using a form of shorthand in his opening sentence (although, later, he does go on to explain more fully what he means). But the main point to note is that he has judged the novel's subject – forensic scientist solves serial murder – too routine to open the review without the addition of that critical twist.

Another straightforward way to begin is with a summing-up of your judgment:

> This is a magical and magisterial production by Adrian Noble: one of the finest accounts I've seen of a magical and magisterial play . . .
> John Peter reviewing *The Tempest* in the *Sunday Times*

> One of the freshest-sounding singles this year has arrived . . .
> Matt Munday reviewing Doris Day's *To Ulrike M* in the *Big Issue*

> *Jackie Brown* is fun . . .
> Alexander Walker in the London *Evening Standard*

You may, however, prefer to create suspense: to keep your readers waiting for both the basic facts and your judgment. One way is to drop them immediately into the heart of the experience.

> Nine men packing shotguns storm the old house at the edge of town. They are there to rout out the women. Teach them a lesson. Kill them.
> Fiona Morrow reviewing Toni Morrison's *Paradise* in *Time Out*

> Inside the Roundhouse at Chalk Farm, shining like a huge paper lantern in the enclosing dark, is this truncated, spiral, vision thing, conspicuously clean, with walls in white nylon and a fresh softwood scent, strong enough to overcome, almost, the smell of old dirt.
> William Feaver reviewing an installation by The Kabakovs in the *Observer*

As long as the image you select is strong, readers will be prepared to wait for a context or an explanation.

Or you might decide to open with the visceral *feel* of the thing you are reviewing:

> A dense, thudding read that pumps its message home with the deliberation of a master sound system . . .
> J B Woolford reviewing Mark Hudson's *The Music in My Head* in *Pride*

Or – this opening is frequently used – you might decide on a teasing or provocative statement:

> The charms of crockery can be overlooked . . .
> Tibor Fischer reviewing Janet Gleeson's *The Arcanum* in the *Mail on Sunday*

> There are not enough sounds on the stage nowadays.
> Susannah Clapp reviewing Nancy Meckler's production of *I Am Yours* in the *Observer*

> Wife swapping will be the main topic of conversation at dinner parties this month.
> Charlie Higson reviewing Ang Lee's *The Ice Storm* in *Red*

Or you might start with a relevant anecdote, personal or otherwise:

Nobody, it seems, bothers to read *Ulysses* nowadays. On a recent *Tea Junction* on Radio 4, the novelist Michael Dobbs remarked that he had yet to meet anyone who had finished it.
John Carey reviewing *James Joyce and Censorship* in the *Sunday Times*

I have come away from gigs exhilarated. I have come away from gigs disappointed. I've even come away from gigs held in a headlock by bouncers.
Barbara Ellen reviewing a Cornershop concert in the *Observer*

Jokes, quotes, questions: a review may begin with any of these. Sooner rather than later, however, you must get round to telling the reader *what* it is you are reviewing.

How to express your opinion

You have written the opening paragraph. Either in it, or shortly after, you have explained what it is you are reviewing. Now for the bulk of the review.

Perhaps the most important point to consider as you continue writing is the need to justify your assertions with illustration, explanation or argument. Except when the word-length is really tight, it is not enough to declare baldly that such-and-such a movie is 'funny'. You need to quote lines or describe a scene illustrating the funniness. The reasons for this are several. First, an example is usually more vivid to read than a simple statement. Second, you may find that, when you search for a suitable example, you are forced to reconsider, modify or even change your assertion.

Third, you owe it to the reader and the work you are reviewing. However informed or intelligent your opinions, you must never believe they are absolute. So, by describing what you find funny, you allow room for readers to conclude that your sense of humour and theirs are different. Similarly, were you to decide that a book was 'a load of macho nonsense', you would need to provide enough evidence of this for your readers to calculate to what extent your idea of nonsense corresponds with theirs.

Should you, therefore, keep repeating 'In my opinion' or 'I felt'? No: a review is transparently an expression of the writer's opinion. You may need to declare an interest. You should, for instance, make it clear if the director of the play you are reviewing is your mother. Or, if reviewing a collection of gay erotic poetry, you might well conclude that your sexuality needed spelling out (even your sex, if your byline left that ambiguous). But to keep insisting 'This is just my opinion' is redundant and faintly annoying.

Next: avoid empty adjectives. 'Brilliant', 'beautiful', 'awful' and so on are the sounds of someone flailing in the dark. Consider *why* you think something is awful (or brilliant, or beautiful or whatever), then tell your readers.

You can even convey a judgment through description alone. Take, for instance, this sentence from a Nicola Barker restaurant review in the *Observer*: 'The meal begins with tubs of steaming hot, ripe-as-all-hell tomato and nippy mint soup with chunks of butter-drenched walnut bread.' All right, that may not be your idea of a tasty, or indeed healthy, hors d'oeuvre, but it's clear, without her spelling it out, that Barker found it delicious.

Praise is a delight to receive but not easy to give. Even experienced critics, reviewing something they have loved, are prone to lose themselves and their readers in a mist of vacuous superlatives. The solution is to be as clear, precise and specific as you can – taking the time to analyse exactly what it was that gave you pleasure.

That said, it is widely agreed that praise is harder to write than knocking copy. A good insult springs from the fingers with such a satisfying elegance. Consider how gratified Mary McCarthy must have felt as she typed this condemnation of fellow writer Lillian Hellman:

> Every word she writes is a lie, including 'and' and 'the'.

Or what about this, from the nineteenth-century critic Eugene Field reviewing a production of *King Lear*:

> He played the King as though under momentary apprehension that someone else was about to play the Ace.

Beware of libel

If you truthfully feel that adverse comment is in order, then by all means go ahead. But do take care that your insults are appropriate and relevant. Insulting a performer's physical appearance, for instance, is relevant only if it has direct bearing on the work. Moreover, as a critic, *you are not immune to the libel laws*.

You do have a defence to the charge, which you share with columnists and satirists. It is known as 'fair comment'. According to this you may, paradoxically, be as *un*fair as you want, so long as whatever you write is your 'honest opinion'. But this is where things get dangerous.

First, opinion is not the same as fact. You would be perfectly entitled, for instance, to write that the crowd scenes in a production of Shakespeare's *Julius Caesar* gave the impression that Rome contained only three plebeians. But were you to write that the crowds were composed of three actors, when in fact they were composed of five, you would have no defence to libel.

Second, if your opinion is way over the top, it might be concluded that it could not be 'honest'. Libel suits against reviewers are rare, but a successful one was brought against a columnist whose comments on the size of an actress's bum were judged not only factually wrong but far too excessive to be 'honest'.

Third, you must not be motivated by malice. Should your bastard of an ex-lover publish a collection of poetry, do not, whatever you do, review it. Were you to write that their sense of rhythm had obviously not improved, you would have no defence to libel.

The fourth test of 'honest opinion' is that you should be commenting on a matter of public interest. This should not usually worry you, since a published work or a public performance is obviously of public interest. But it does raise another, non-legal, question. Critics disagree about this, but to me it seems there is little point in slamming artists so obscure that, were it not for your reviewing their work, your readers would be blithely unaware of them. Would it not be better to leave them in obscurity?

Name the artist

Condemning or praising, you should usually name the people singled out. This may seem obvious if the artist in question is a famous chef, the lead singer in a band, the star of a show, the author of a book. But it also applies to translators, arrangers, set designers and so on. If you think the lighting made an important contribution to a ballet, name the designer.

For actors, there are two conventions, depending on the structure of the sentence. If it is structured with the actor given more importance than the role, then you simply name him as you would any other artist whose work you were mentioning. If, however, it is the role that has most importance in the sentence, then the actor's name is usually inserted in brackets: 'Ulysses Jackson (Peter Fonda) works as a beekeeper in the tupelo marshes of rural Florida . . .'

Spoiling the suspense

At the end of Agatha Christie's theatrical whodunnit *The Mousetrap*, audiences are asked to keep the murderer's identity a secret so as not to spoil the suspense for those who have yet to see the play. Should critics generally refrain from revealing twists, surprises and denouements?

There are two schools of thought about this. The first holds that of course they should, that anything else would wreck the enjoyment of potential audiences and readers. The second holds that, since a review is not an advertising trailer, it is entirely legitimate to reveal whatever the critic likes. This is something you will need to decide for yourself. (When it comes to film reviews, however, the dilemma may soon become obsolete, with audiences ever more inclined to post plot-spoilers on social media even as they're watching.)

Endings

The end of a review is usually a summing-up of the critic's opinion:

> Marling's fifth [album] takes vast steps forward musically, as ever. It's more defiant and distinct than anything she's done before, testament to her first go at self-production. But what really sets it apart from her catalogue is her desire to break the cycle, to let go and let herself be young. Next verse? It's anyone's guess, including hers.
> Laura Snapes reviewing Laura Marling's *Short Movie* album in *Uncut*

> In truth, this is a barmy little sketch posing as a revolutionary satire.
> Lloyd Evans reviewing the play *Radiant Vermin* in the *Spectator*

> This is not a novel to be tossed aside lightly. It should be thrown with great force.
> Dorothy Parker

No rules dictate this formulation. But skim as many reviews as you like and you will see that they might as well. In other words, you may end a review in whatever way you see fit but, if you find it *difficult* to end, then summing up your opinion is as good a solution as any. Besides, you will make life easier for lazy or hard-pressed readers, who know that skipping to the end of a review will usually tell them, if nothing else, whether to get their wallet out.

Online reviews

For an in-depth account of writing for the internet, read the chapters on writing for digital publication (pages 117–49). If you want to become a reviewer, however, you should also bear in mind that there are several kinds of online review.

The first occupies the same professional space as most print reviews. Not only has the writer been paid but the review has been commissioned and overseen by an editor. In some cases, this kind of review will be the electronic version of one that has already appeared in print; in other cases, it will have been written especially for the internet.

But many of the blogs that review music, movies, books, etc are run and/or contributed to by enthusiastic amateurs – critics who work for love, not money. Also unpaid are most of the reviews found on retail sites such as Amazon.

This *need* not mean that such reviews are incompetent, ill-informed or generally worthless. People who post reviews for free may still have expertise, integrity and passion and many of the non-commercial blogs, in particular, are excellent. It's also the case that retailers find 'customer reviews' invaluable; research suggests that they influence online shoppers more strongly than ads do.

But the status of unsolicited reviews is not universally high. The most prolific online book reviewers, for instance, may post as many as one review a day, which raises doubts about the thoroughness with which they read the books in question. Online reviewers have also been known to puff their own products – books, hotels – under a pseudonym. And, for a modest fee, there are companies that will write fake reviews to order.

Admittedly, print reviews can also be deceptive. In the 1960s Anthony Burgess wrote a perversely enticing review of a novel that he himself had written under the *nom de plume* Joseph Kell. 'This is a dirty book,' he wrote in the *Yorkshire Post*. 'It may well make some people sick, and those of my readers with tender stomachs are advised to let it alone.' By and large, however, there are too many checks on the authenticity of print reviews to allow that kind of concealed self-promotion.

Although aspiring reviewers might want to *practise* by posting unsolicited reviews on the internet, such publication is unlikely to count for much on their curriculum vitae.

How to get in

To become the regular film critic for a national paper or glossy magazine takes time, experience and contacts. The same is true should you wish to become a regular critic of any sort for a prestigious, well-paying media outlet. Such jobs are rarely available to young or inexperienced journalists. Moreover, reviewers are not, in general, among the best-paid journalists. They get to see a lot of movies, keep a lot of CDs and books but, even if they have the luck to be on a salary or long-term contract, they are unlikely to become millionaires.

There is more bad news. Because so many young writers are interested in the arts, the competition for reviewing work is intense. But there is good news too.

Youth can work to your advantage. Most publications prefer to have younger journalists reviewing pop music, video games, comedy etc. Less obviously, a literary editor may specifically want a young reviewer for a book aimed at the youth market or written by a young author.

Specialist knowledge or special experience can also be a useful springboard. If, for instance, you know all there is to know about drum'n'bass, then you are in a stronger position than someone with casual, generalised musical knowledge. Similarly, if you have experience of accounting, snowboarding, being the child of alcoholic parents or whatever, you have a good case to put to a literary editor with a book on one of those subjects awaiting review. Or, if you live outside of London and know your way round the local music, theatre, dance, club or art scene, you could be useful to arts editors fed up with trying to persuade staff journalists to travel.

The crucial thing is to keep abreast of what is happening in your chosen field; by and large editors know about the immediate and the mainstream. Ask publishers to send you their catalogues. Keep in touch with your local theatres, music venues, clubs. Read specialist publications. Surf the internet. Hang out with people who work in the arts. And, if you get a job as a sub, editorial assistant or reporter, but would like to be writing reviews as well or instead, make frequent visits to the arts desk to enquire about what is coming up.

Finally, although you should study the style and approach of whatever publication you would like to review for, you should never, ever, try to reproduce its critics' opinions. Your views, your take on things, are what matter – both to commissioning editors and to yourself. They are why people will want to employ you. They are what give you your individual voice. They are why you want to be a critic.

The ways in to reviewing may be obscure and hard to locate but, if you look hard enough, they are there.

Why bother?

The question is: why bother?

If you want to be a hero, do not become a critic. Creative artists hate critics. Readers delight in arguing with them. History loves looking back at them and sneering at what they got wrong. The only reason to write reviews is that you enjoy the art or entertainment form about which you write, enjoy being forced to consider why such a thing works and such a thing does not, enjoy trying to convey your experience in words.

If, when you were a child, someone had told you that you could earn money by cuddling up with a succession of books; sitting transfixed in the cinema; going to the theatre, the ballet, the opera, rock concerts; eating out in restaurants; watching television; watching DVDs; listening to CDs: what would have been your reaction? If you would have shrugged, forget reviewing. If you would have laughed with amazement, go for it.

Two reviews

Adam Mars-Jones reviewing Sebastian Barry's novel *The Whereabouts of Eneas McNulty* in the *Observer*:

> Sebastian Barry's new novel is so full of magnetising beauty that it all but harasses a reader into submission. You can try to protest, to say, 'I'm a reader and you're a book, can we not keep this on a professional basis?' but the book won't have it so. *The Whereabouts of Eneas McNulty* is Barry's first novel for 10 years, and during that decade he has made a major mark with his plays, but in these pages he seems most like a poet. Many sentences seem actively to yearn for an uneven right-hand margin to point up their rhythms and designs: 'The cold desert in his mind's eye floods with the thousand small white flowers that are the afterlife of rainfall.'
>
> Eneas McNulty is born in Sligo at the turn of the century, first child of a Catholic jobbing tailor, who met his seamstress wife-to-be in the asylum where he worked running up clothing for the inmates. Eneas is dispossessed for the first time when more children come along, but is consoled by friendship with an older boy, Jonno Lynch.
>
> At 16, for no reason except the need to find a place for himself, and a vague desire to rescue poor, suffering France, Eneas joins the British Merchant navy. His taking of the King's shilling is not a political decision: in a striking phrase applied to the proprietor of the Great Western Hotel in Athlone, he – and the book which contains him – might be described as being 'above politics and beneath neutrality'.
>
> After the war Eneas compounds his error of affiliation by joining the Royal Irish Constabulary and brands himself, in the changing political climate, definitively traitor. He isn't so stupid as not to know 'why there are places in the peelers when there are places nowhere else' but he can hardly predict the slow fuse of hatred that will follow him down the decades. Sentence of death is confirmed by Jonno, by the dear friend estranged. Eneas becomes a sort of sorrowful human comet, travelling in a highly elliptical orbit far from Sligo, in search of a place and an occupation – fishing, farming, digging – but returning at long intervals to whizz, grieving, past his family. He must part from the woman he loves, and never finds a substitute for her. Eneas may be named after a hero whose wanderings were ordained and finally rewarded, but he himself finds no home to replace the one he lost.
>
> If Barry's prose is poetry carried on by other means, he is an unfashionable sort of poet, drawing images almost exclusively from the natural world, seen as a teeming library of images, mainly redemptive: 'The salmon is as

clean as a pig in its nature, though unlike the pig it will not lie down in the dirt that men force on it.'

Eneas isn't an articulate man as the world sees it, but like all the characters in the book he has his own eloquence. Sweetly reproached by his pappy for his poor performance as a correspondent, he replies wryly: 'The writing hand is a rusty hand, that's true.' There are times when Barry misses blarney by only a leprechaun's whisker – when it occurs to Eneas that his pappy is 'a bit of a fool, a bit of a colossal fool' – but there's no doubt that the book is a stylistic triumph. And yet the truth is that the infinite distinction of the writing becomes limitation, almost, since the primal delight adheres to the separate sentences rather than the story they carry. The urge to read on is not really a desire to know what happens to the hero next, but to see what new marvels of phrasing Barry will breed from his stock of pet words.

Eneas's character is distinctly idealised, suffering and bewildered but exempted from serious internal tensions. He meets hatred with weariness but without embitterment. He is less an exile than an involuntary citizen of the world. He suffers mightily, but the prose in which his days and doings are suspended is balm for the reader if not for him. Readers of the book, gratified, selfish, may wish its hero well in a dim sort of way, but would happily see Eneas driven to the top of the barest crag, if that would guarantee his being struck a few thousand more times by the loving light-ning of his maker's language.
Observer, 15 March 1998

The structure of this is classic. It opens by jumping forward with the visceral *feel* of the book (while deftly telling, or reminding, readers who the author is), then steps back to provide an outline of the plot and to hint at the themes. This is followed by the bulk of the assessment, helpfully illustrated with quotations. It makes both negative and positive points, but ends on the one that Mars-Jones thinks most important (with which he also opened the review): that the novel's language is beautiful.

His own language is precise and vivid, too. Look, for instance, at that final sentence. And notice how, as an *Observer* writer, he compliments his readers by assuming they have heard of the wandering Trojan hero Aeneas and will recog-nise the quotation about the relationship of war to diplomacy that he echoes in 'If Barry's prose is poetry carried on by other means . . .' Most important, though, is that the review provides such a potent *sense* of the novel that readers will know very well, by the end, whether or not they want to read it.

Sylvia Patterson on Tori Amos's album *From the Choirgirl Hotel* in *Frank*:

She is 34 and still believes in fairies. She was raped at gunpoint and still believes in love. She is Tori Amos, 'bonkers banshee piano woman', purveyor of lyrical paeans to the joys of giving God a blow job, and a multi-million-selling 'cult' artiste with the sort of fame which spawns devoted 'fans' who hide in bushes with guns. Thus, as with all extremists, many people (especially boys) cannot be doing with Tori Amos, for she is a wailing siren who sings about blood clots running down your inner thighs – but, of course, these males are crybaby saps who are terrified of women's (sometimes literal) innards.

This time, however, after the chilling 1996 *Boys for Pele* (which signalled 'a change in my relationship with men for good'), she comes to us a glittery-eyed newlywed. But don't be looking for 'love-is-a-many-splendoured-thing' here. She is also a soul-shattered mother-to-be who miscarried her baby in 1997. *From the Choirgirl Hotel* is the story of how she coped and how she didn't and how, in the end, she found a brand-new passion for Life. And how, while she was at it, she found herself a band of musicianly gifted snooksters with whom she expanded her spiky piano dramatics into whole new dimensions of soundscape terror and epic gorgeousness. Which, at least once (on the baying *Cruel*), has turned her into Patti Smith guesting on a particularly 'dark' Tricky song.

This is Amos's shock-free album, featuring no artwork treats like piglets being suckled on her breast (as she did inside *Boys for Pele*); on this sleeve she floats in blackness, with her hands engaged in some flaky-fingered Ted Rogers '321' impersonation (but more likely the magic signalling of Inca binary charms, or some such). So, she's free, and, in freedom, brings us her version of the ubiquitous late-90s epic with a different kind of lyric: 'She's addicted to nicotine patches' goes the hairy *Spark*; 'She's afraid of a light in the dark . . . but she couldn't keep baby alive.' And in *Playboy Mommy* she sings to the spirit of what she was sure was going to be her daughter: 'Don't judge me so harsh little girl . . . you gotta playboy mommy.'

It's sorrow set, however, to some of the most beautiful sounds Amos has ever conjured from her kaleidoscopic mind: the rousing *Raspberry Swirl*, the mournful loveliness of *Liquid Diamonds*, the frankly hysterical *She's Your Cocaine* and the goose-bump caper of *Northern Lad* which breaks your heart in 47 places and then makes you want to leap naked off the top of an Icelandic volcano brimful of finest Viking vodka.

Her voice, too, has found a new fandango to dance. The vocal gymnastics of *Hotel* are berserk to behold, before she coos, 'I'm still alive . . . I'm still alive . . . I'm still alive.' Tori Amos is, in actual fact, one of those rare people who is Truly Alive; positively exploding, in fact, with life. It is this which makes her 'mad', which is to say she has a personality, big ideas, a bigger heart, and a wise head and something to say about rock'n'roll and pain and sacrifice and joy. *From the Choirgirl Hotel* is the first Tori Amos album you can dance to (on the right kind of drugs). You could even have sex to it and not feel squiffy afterwards. It is more P J Harvey and Portishead than Kate Bush, and the furthest away from the 'madwoman-with-a-piano' stereotype she has ever been; it's over the lone-piano wall into the multi-layered atmospheric pool of Joni Mitchell and the technology of Massive Attack. And, like all the best ideas, you wonder why she didn't think of it before.

Frank, June 1998

Although this is very different in voice from Adam Mars-Jones's review above, it shares with it the power to make readers experience what the reviewer experienced, feel the reviewer's enthusiasm and know, by the end, whether or not the work of art is their kind of thing. This review opens by talking, at length, about the artist: not only because the facts of her life are attention-grabbing but because the album is, in effect, a chapter of her autobiography. The assessment component which follows is apparently nothing but positive, but the odd tongue-in-cheek phrase – 'more likely the magic signalling of Inca binary charms, or some such' – concedes that the album might sometimes veer towards pretentiousness.

Patterson's language is sometimes more inventive than correct – 'musicianly gifted snooksters' – but never incomprehensible. And although she does, at one point, describe Amos's 'sounds' as 'beautiful', she immediately specifies what she means: 'the goose-bump caper of *Northern Lad* which breaks your heart in 47 places ...' (The side-swipes at 'boys' and 'crybaby' men in the opening paragraph are there at least in part because *Frank* was a magazine aimed at women.)

6
Writing for digital publication – shortform

Tim Holmes

'Writing for the website has fundamentally changed how I write in print'
Ta-Nehisi Coates

With the excellent advice contained in the rest of this book, why have two chapters devoted specially to writing for digital publication? Well-written journalism is well-written journalism wherever it appears and what is considered good in print will also be considered good when paper is replaced by the screen of a computer, a tablet, a mobile or even a smart watch.

This is true, but only if you think of digitally published content as a direct analogue of what appears in print: a news story lifted straight from the original word-processing file and pasted into a content-management system; a feature converted from InDesign to a pdf file and posted to a hosting service like issuu. com. These seem to be straightforward examples where no further knowledge or skill need be applied to the writing and that might well be the case – but only if you are writing for a backward-looking organisation and you don't mind the fact that although you potentially have a global readership your work will get lost.

As far as working for a backward-looking organisation is concerned, the idea of not having to add anything to the word-processing file once the story is written would be a dead giveaway. Media organisations now realise that publishing for digital consumption is a new realm, with its own set of practices. The *Guardian*, for example, has embraced digital publication and helped to develop new techniques requiring a broader set of skills from writers and production journalists. As *Guardian* sub Barbara Harper says:

> A subeditor preparing an article for our website will, among other things, be expected to write headlines that are optimised for search engines so the article can be easily seen online, add keywords to make sure it appears in the right places on the website, create packages to direct readers to related

articles, embed links, attach pictures, add videos and think about how the article will look when it is accessed on mobile phones and other digital platforms.[1]

Her colleague Charlotte Baxter adds:

> Working online, we choose and upload pictures and add keywords – to index a piece within the guardian.co.uk site – and links, trying to use primary sources where possible.[2]

Despite its financial situation (the organisation expected to lose £20m in 2015[3]) and years of job cuts (in 2012 Guardian Media Group was looking to cut 100 journalists from its payroll[4]), the *Guardian* is still a relatively large and well-staffed organisation with specialist subeditors and production journalists to tweak work provided by specialist writers. The same financial and employment pressures, however, are evident throughout the media industries and it is normal practice for reporters and feature writers to undertake the kind of work previously handled by production staff.

In effect this is an interesting evolution of 'convergence'. When the term was coined to describe the ways in which media technologies appeared to be merging, many thought the result would be a reporter burdened with video and still cameras, an audio recorder and a portable computer for writing. Of course this has happened but since all the equipment has been shrunk to the size of a smartphone it's not much of a physical burden.

More importantly, the idea of convergence has been reconceptualised, so that cultural scholar Henry Jenkins can say:

> Convergence should not be understood primarily as a technological process bringing together multiple media functions within the same devices. Instead, convergence represents a cultural shift as consumers are encouraged to seek out new information and make connections among dispersed media content.[5]

What this means for journalists is that the *technological* aspect of convergence – the creation and presentation of moving images, photographs, sound and the written word on one universal device rather than multiple specialised devices – is no longer the key point. More important is the realisation that the reader is now an active agent in the process of convergence, seeking out and combining different forms of content in order to create a richer experience. We know this to be true because people now use social media to comment on television programmes – the *second screen* phenomenon; likewise, it has become common for readers to use Facebook or Twitter to comment on pieces they have read, and journalism websites positively encourage readers to share by providing buttons for social media as well as space for comments.

The inevitable corollary of this is that the journalist must seek out the reader, rather than the reader seeking the writer. To access the truth of this, just answer one question: how do you find things online?

An obvious answer will be 'I use Google', which is what most people would say. But think further about how you use Google most of the time: in the context of journalism it's not usually to find a specific article by a specific writer; it's more likely to be a more general inquiry within a topic – *climate change*, say, or *Cheryl Fernandez-Versini*. Making your writing easier to find by increasing its search-ability is just one of the considerations a twenty-first-century journalist has to bear in mind, and we will look at how to maximise the chances of success later in this chapter.

If you make a more considered list of the ways that you find content online – or of the ways that online content finds you – it's likely to include Facebook, Twitter, Instagram, Pinterest and other forms of social media, as well as friends, acquaintances or even total strangers sending you links to things they think you will find funny, interesting or profitable (for them, most likely).

When information is abundant – infinite even – guides and filters become more valuable, but what links these modes of discovery? Two elements stand out immediately: they must be *short* and they must compete for *attention*.

To take the latter first, back in 1997 Michael Goldhaber identified a new kind of capital, very different from the financial capital that has troubled old-style publishing since the world wide web went mainstream and started to eat established media's dinner. His conference paper *The Attention Economy and the Net* outlined the principles of the new paradigm: if information is ubiquitous, getting people to spend their limited amount of attention on any particular piece of information becomes increasingly important because, 'economies are governed by what is scarce, and information, especially on the Net, is not only abundant, but overflowing' whereas 'Attention, at least the kind we care about, is an intrinsically scarce resource.'[6]

If you, the writer, can attract the reader's attention in a universe of competing attention seekers you will have achieved something valuable. This is not an end in itself, merely a means to an end; but without the ability to start conversations with your potential readership community in one medium (social) about other media (website, print), your success as a writer is likely to flag and fail – without the ability to attract attention your story will not take off.

The ability to measure everything online (not just how many people click on your story but how long they stay there, where they were directed from, where they are from in the world, what device they used to access it) has taken a central place in publishing and thus in journalism. It is not a measure of worth but a measure of popularity and while those two values do not necessarily have a direct correlation, the fact that metrics are given such emphasis is not so much part of what Martin Heidegger might characterise as a journalistic Verfallsgeschichte – a narrative or history of decline – as an accepted fact of life for a writer.

Engagement with the community of readers, the audience, is a two-way process and the very fact of engagement can change the way a journalist writes – at least, Ta-Nehesi Coates believes so. Coates's book *Between the World and Me* was published to considerable acclaim in 2015 but before that he won an award for his essay *Fear of a Black President*[7], published in the *Atlantic* in September 2012. After receiving the prize he wrote on his blog:

> Writing for the website has fundamentally changed how I write in print. . . . This space is my notebook. But in the borders and outside the margins you can see the added scribblings and post-its authored by The Horde . . .[8]

Coates's point here is that people who leave comments (The Horde) help him to be a better journalist by directing him to new sources of information, by correcting his understanding of philosophy and his translations from French. The blog gives him the opportunity to try out ideas and have a first run at writing and the readers who engage with the blog help to sharpen his understanding and increase his knowledge.

The blog post in which he thanks The Horde is just 273 words long. As James Bennett wrote (also in the *Atlantic* and with reference to Coates): 'As journalism and its distribution through the web evolve, the most meaningful distinction is turning out to be not short versus long but good versus bad.'[9]

Nevertheless, in looking at writing for digital publication short is a very good place to start, not because people will not read lengthy journalism on a screen – they will, as the next chapter shows – but because as with news writing, short is a good way to condense meaning. Not short like a news piece with its pyramidal structure and multiple paragraphs but *really* short like a tweet of 140 characters.

Learn to love Twitter

Twitter is a fantastic tool for journalists – if you doubt that, just look at the number of journalists and news organisations who use it. At one end of the scale it represents the homogenisation of communication hierarchies with all contributors operating at the same level of importance; at the other it eradicates the gatekeeping function of journalism in favour of instantaneous democratic publication:

- An individual can let the world know about his fashion faux pas: 'It's 12.35pm. Just discovered I've been walking round for three hours with my right trouser leg tucked into my sock from cycling to work', Josh Halliday 28 July 2015 (Halliday is also a reporter on the *Guardian*).
- A café can let potential customers know about a midday treat: 'Lunchtime yeh! Bacon, Halloumi & caramelised onion, yup', Deli a GoGo City, 28 July 2015.
- A media organisation can follow up the story of a civil outrage: 'Mexico found 129 bodies in mass graves in 10 months – but none were the missing 43 students', *Vice News*, 27 July 2015.
- A news organisation can break a story: 'Two journalists killed in Somalia in car bomb attack on hotel', *Guardian*, 28 July 2015.

These tweets show four of the most important modes of social media: self-expression, promotion, investigation/follow-up and information/breaking news. The modes are not mutually exclusive and journalists will find themselves using each mode on different occasions. Only the first of these examples came without a shortened url link to carry potential customers/readers through to a website with more information/the full story.

However, it's important to define success in this context and also to decide how to present yourself to the world. By that I mean choosing a reasonable Twitter handle (name) and completing the user profile. The name does not have to be entirely sensible but if you want your work to be taken seriously you might be better off as @JohnJournalist than @TinkyWinkyDoodle. Most of the straight-forward renditions of first and second names are likely to have been taken but you can add a number (@JohnJournalist555) or include initials (@John VZJournalist). If you are tweeting as an official employee you will probably have to comply with a house style and a code of practice; if as yourself but sometimes tweeting work-related content, you might include a disclaimer in your profile such as 'all views my own'.

Even though there is no great secret about how to write a good tweet (short, to the point, conversational, interesting, clever where appropriate, funny if possible), it is informative to observe the way other journalists present themselves in and out of their 'official' roles. Spend some time following them and analyse every element of their posts – the words chosen, the expressions employed, the mode of addressing the reader, the mode of use and the links. For example:

- @jo_elvin (101,000 followers) is the editor of *Glamour* and she successfully combines tweets about her personal life with tweets to do with the magazine. Personal example: 'Husband is cooking. I am drinking. I feel this is the natural order of things'; professional example: 'It's Glamour

Day! August Glamour out now. Here's a sneak peek, my editor's letter http://bit.ly/elvin01'.

- Rory Cellan-Jones, the BBC's technology correspondent, has two accounts: @ruskin147 (163,000 followers) is nominally his personal account but among the pictures of his dog and his home-baked loaves there's plenty of technology-related material; his official account @BBCRoryCJ (145,000 followers) is very similar but without the collie and bread. Ruskin example: 'Big weekend of family celebration means lots of baking – @diane1859 famous cheesecake, my new Nigella chocolate cake' (above picture of cake); BBCRory example: 'Windows 10 launches today – here's my crash course http://bit.ly/rorycj01'.

- Emma Barnett (@Emmabarnett, 36,900 followers) combines being women's editor of the *Telegraph* with presenting BBC 5 Live's *Hit List* and hosting *Woman's Hour* on Radio 4 – there's so much going on in that combination of roles that she is never at a loss for professional tweetable material but she includes her own opinions too. Personal/professional example: 'anyone else seen disgraceful attempt by @CafeRougeTweet to milk #Calais HUMANITARIAN crisis? http://bit.ly/emmab01'.

- @Tomstandage (18,700 followers) is deputy editor of the *Economist* and author of many excellent books including *The Victorian Internet*, a history of telegraphy; his Twitter feed has a strong tech/media bias but encompasses many of his other interests. Personal example: 'Epic #Hyperlapse video by @kirstinmckee shows our boat trip to lunch yesterday (you can see the table at the end) http://bit.ly/1heAp3n'; professional example: 'Has the world reached peak alcohol? Consumption per capita is down: http://www.economist.com/news/business/21659754-booze-around-world'.

- Also look at @TheEconomist (9.73 million followers) as an example of how to tweet links to articles: 'Nearly 20m Indians reach the legal drinking annually. Foreign booze firms stand to benefit http://econ.st/1gmIOlh' and 'Benson, England's best-loved fish, died on this day in 2009, aged about 25. Read our obituary http://econ.st/1IqmKvR' are two beguiling examples that demonstrate the title's range and variety of content.

These are just five examples and you should find your own set of accounts to follow; when you look at them, note not only how posts are worded but also the additional material included – links, photographs, video, audio, infographics, charts. You will also find that many tweets include the handles of other Twitter users (an example from Tom Standage: '@charlesarthur @jeffjarvis @GeorgeBouras Did you see this essay on the moral case against advertising? http://www.abc.net.au/religion/articles/2015/07/14/4273200.htm . . . via @azeem'), creating a public conversation between selected individuals. All of these elements go towards making your own Twitter style.

The other factor referred to above, deciding what success means, is even more important. Clearly the more followers you have, the more readers you can reach but collecting followers in itself does not mean a great deal. More relevant are how engaged those followers are, and what they do when they read your tweets – do they click on the link, improving the metrics on your content? Do they retweet, spreading the material among their own network? Do they add a comment, contributing to interaction with your readership community and perhaps adding value in the way Ta-Nehisi Coates suggests? Establish your own values and measure progress against them.

Twitter advice

https://support.twitter.com/articles/69214

http://bit.ly/tweets01

http://bit.ly/tweets02

Face up to Facebook

Good and journalism-friendly though Twitter is, its 302 million monthly users (sending 500 million tweets per day)[10] cannot compare with Facebook's 1.44 billion monthly users (936 million daily users)[11] for sheer scale and reach. If you are going to practise social journalism, you cannot do so without Facebook.

As far as is possible you should make your social media persona consistent through all the various iterations and platforms – if you are @JohnJournalist, try to be John Journalist on Facebook. It might be an idea to scope out the naming possibilities on all the social platforms you intend to use before making a decision. The other important choice, as with Twitter, is to decide the balance between personal and professional or whether it would be better to have separate accounts for work and play. Sometimes a journalist's persona will be such that work and play naturally fall together but this is exceptional.

Usefully, Facebook has published several articles about how media organisations and individual journalists can make best use of the platform, including plenty of tips about how to improve storytelling and augment reporting. Rather than paraphrase this expert advice I am going to follow Jeff Jarvis's digital dictum ('Cover what you do best. Link to the rest.' (http://bit.ly/jarvislink)) by including links to these pages below. It is worth noting, however, that a conversational and personal tone is recommended, and the fundamental rule of journalism about making every word count still applies.

Facebook advice

http://bit.ly/fbadvice01

http://bit.ly/fbadvice02

http://bit.ly/fbadvice03

Writing for pictures: Instagram & Pinterest

It might seem odd to have a section about social media platforms that rely on the visual for their interest but – leaving aside the fact that both can be useful for sourcing images or even stories, not to mention their 300 million[12] and 72.8 million[13] users respectively – as all journalists should know, pictures require captions and understanding how to write good captions is a merchandise more precious than rubies (Proverbs 3:15). Furthermore, both platforms can be used by writers, in different ways, to create narratives to accompany single pictures (Instagram) or boards of images (Pinterest). Just as with other social media, users can choose to *like* images and can engage further by sharing them and posting comments.

Instagram allows users to post captions of up to 2,000 characters, which is more than enough to provide context for the image and place it within a narrative relevant to either an individual journalist, a single story or a media organisation. *National Geographic* (natgeo) is a natural fit, given the magazine's emphasis on stunning photography. See if you can imagine the image described by this caption:

> <u>natgeo</u> Midnight sun on north west Svalbard and the light starts to get better. We're working on a small ice strengthened vessel called Havsel, Shown here at anchor in a sheltered bay in front of a glacier. To make the most of the lighting conditions . . .

The rest of the caption says that with the support of the ship's crew, photographer Nick Cobbing turned day to night because the harsh light of the afternoon is better for sleeping while the quality light of the night is better for photography and filming. Check out the whole thing at: http://bit.ly/1K0wL43.

Note how the caption itself is not a direct plug for *National Geographic* or for the photographer – it sets a scene and tells a story. This is very important for emotional engagement: readers feel as though they are learning something and being allowed in on a privileged view. Three days after posting it had received 388,000 likes and 937 comments.

Compare it with this example from *Time* magazine. The photograph shows a small boy in a white interior, an ornate mirror above him, an open door through to a kitchen to his right; he is sitting on a French stool wearing just shorts and a red cape; the picture is both mundane and somehow unsettling. (Unfortunately it is not possible to reproduce the whole caption because of reproduction issues with the rights holders.) The post began:

> <u>time</u> It's time to rethink what it means to be exceptional. "Somewhere between the self-esteem building of going for the gold and the self-esteem crushing of the Ivy-or-die ethos there has to be a place where kids can breathe, where they can have the freedom to do what they love . . ."

The remainder of the caption précised a feature by Jeffrey Kluger that examined how the definition of achievement in childhood is being discussed and changed. For the full experience check out https://instagram.com/p/5mgWbbK6wX/?taken-by=time.

This *is* a direct plug for the then-current issue of the magazine but it focuses on a story that is likely to resonate with many parents; the words promise thoughtful and perhaps controversial content. Four days after being published it had received 16,700 likes and attracted 285 comments – good figures but nowhere near as good as the example above.

Finally, Instagram images can be deployed as editorial material in themselves. *Time Out London* did just this with a graphic showing the layout of the Lovebox festival – a simple stylised map with a numbered key. The caption read:

> <u>timeoutlondon</u> Who's heading to#Lovebox? Here's a map for you to screenshot and keep. // 1 - Main Stage // 2 - West Stage // 3 - Big Top // 4 - Elrow // 5 - Despacio // 6 - Corona Sunsets // 7 - The Voicebox // 8 - The Bandstand // 9 - Bump Roller Disco // 10 - The Vegas Bar[14]

The idea seems quite useful but the image received only 192 likes and a handful of comments, one of which read: 'Carlsberg don't make maps, but if they did. . . It'd be a lot fucking better than this!' This is the other side of the two-way conversation – if people don't like the content you have posted, you'll know all about it.

Pinterest, although not so widely used as Instagram, has established itself as a way for media organisations to extend their brands; many magazines and newspapers have accounts and set up *boards* (themed collections of images). We have already looked at *Glamour* magazine in other contexts, so it is interesting to look at their Pinterest; as you might expect from the UK's best-selling women's magazine, it has attracted a decent number of followers (597,078) but only three likes. By contrast *Cosmopolitan*, which does not have as large a circulation, has 668,849 followers and 389 likes; *Vice* magazine, which caters for a very digitally savvy readership, has a mere 8,171 followers but 1,198 likes (all figures correct in July 2015).

This raises a crucial point for anyone writing for digital publication: the publishing strategy must be correct and appropriate. *Cosmo's* readers clearly like Pinterest much more than *Vice's*, so that is where effort should be expended. On the other hand *Vice* can boast 1.4 million Facebook shares, 471,000 Twitter followers, 1 million YouTube subscribers and 421,000 Google+ followers; it can tailor its strategy appropriately.

Engagement on Pinterest takes several forms: the account can be followed, individual boards can be followed, images can be liked, commented on and repinned (ie copied onto someone else's board), the latter being the ultimate accolade. When it comes to words, each image can have a headline and a caption and the image itself can show a link back to the publication's website or to a retail website from where the reader can buy, for example, fashion items.

To take an image from *Cosmo's* fashion board as an example, in the last week of July 2015 we find a picture of model Rosie Huntingdon-Whiteley standing in a garden wearing a short checked dress; the headline reads 'What the stars are wearing at Paris Haute Couture Fashion Week' and the caption is 'HOW cute is Rosie HW's checked mini? The star wore the dress to watch Christian Dior's AW15 Haute Couture show.' This picture had been repinned 20 times and liked by four.

As a writer, therefore, there are several opportunities to make an impact:

- Create good names for your boards: *Red* magazine (834,116 followers) does this simply but well – 'Nice Food' would say something but 'Dinner Party Recipe Ideas' is more useful and more searchable; 'Rented Home Decorating Ideas' will resonate with generation rent.
- Don't forget the referral link – if it goes to someone else's site it's an important form of credit, if it goes to your own it adds readers and/or revenue.
- Create an interesting, searchable headline that includes important keywords – just look at the examples above to see how that works[15]* (we look at improving searchability below).
- Write an informative/intriguing/amusing/insightful caption that also includes keywords – 'Rosie HW . . . Christian Dior . . . Haute Couture'.
- Ask a question – there is some evidence[16] that framing your caption as a question that demands an answer from readers is an effective way to increase engagement and response.

There is another aspect of writing for Pinterest that is often overlooked: by creating a board of themed images you also have the opportunity of creating a narrative thread that links the board together and makes it more than the sum of its parts. Students at Cardiff University experimented with this very effectively during their work on course magazine *Grill & Barrel*; their first boards were colourful and interesting (eg https://www.pinterest.com/grillandbarrel/bangin-bottle-caps/) but the images were treated as separate items linked only by the overall theme. Later, however, they put together boards that told a story – this one about beer brands that have endured works like a feature: https://www.pinterest.com/grillandbarrel/ye-olde-beers/.

Instagram & Pinterest advice

http://bit.ly/instadvice01

http://bit.ly/instadvice02

http://bit.ly/instadvice03

http://bit.ly/pinadvice01

http://bit.ly/pinadvice02

http://bit.ly/pinadvice03

Tags, #hashtags & timing

The examples above feature a few different formatting elements – the tagging @ format identifies and links to an account and the hashtag # format identifies a genre of content, allows related content to be aggregated into a single feed and converts the word or words that follow into a searchable link. Hashtags have been adopted by many social platforms as well as Instagram and Pinterest – Twitter, Facebook, Google+, Tumblr (via a special 'Tag' section) and Vine. WhatsApp users include hashtags but they do not have an aggregating function. Snapchat has a slightly similar feature called Our Story, though it only works for groups in a specific location.

Crafting a good #hashtag is as much of an art as caption writing and there are some useful rules to observe:

- Do not include spaces; if you want to use a phrase the words must be run together; they can be capitalised (#CardiffTrained) but mixing upper and lowercase letters will not affect search results (#cardifftrained will achieve the same result).
- Numbers work fine but punctuation does not; the operative part of #time'swingedchariot will be reduced to #time; characters like & are not recognised either.

- Do not use too many hashtags in a single post; between one and three achieve best results.
- Make them relevant – think about the key words that people are searching for; check which hashtags are trending but only adopt them if they are appropriate. https://www.hashtags.org/ and Twitter itself will show you what is trending (#YorkshireDay and #BlueMoon are the top two as I write).

Hashtags can also allow you to publish a long narrative as a collection of 140-character instalments. Serial publication is nothing new – Charles Dickens would recognise the principle – but this is an extreme form. Joshua Clover used the technique to publish a story about how and why he resigned from *Spin* magazine – check it out in this Storify aggregation: https://storify.com/bradshoup/how-i-quit-spin.

One other really important factor to bear in mind when devising a digital strategy is timing – when will you release your tweet/Facebook update/Instagram image? By when I mean what time(s) of day, what day(s) of the week, how many a month – every readership community will have times when it is more attentive to your messages and when it is not so attentive. This could be a result of working patterns (lunch break), information needs at specific hours (a recipe for supper), commuting arrangements (train or bus journeys), holiday travel (leisure reading) and so on; without a clear idea of *when* your readership community wants content as well as *what* it wants, much of your effort will be lost in the digital smog.

Blogging[17]

Blogging is one of those things that come and go in a cycle of digital fashion-ability, not least because social media perform some of the same functions. However, many journalists still blog and it can be an excellent way to raise your profile as a journalist, especially if you cover a specialised field; some also use it as a form of column writing. There are many platforms to choose from: of the free ones Wordpress is currently an industry standard, Tumblr makes incorporating audio and video super-simple and Blogger is Google's reliable offering.

As a writing practice, blogging encompasses everything from rambling, ego-maniacal conspiracy theorisation to haikus but journalists who blog should draw on the basics of journalism:

- Have a *very* clear idea of whom you are writing for and what they want to know; developing a specialism and demonstrating your expertise is hugely advantageous in making your blog stand out from the crowd.

- Have something to say and research to back it up.
- Work on creating an effective, appealing and informative headline.
- Craft a great intro and organise the rest into a clear narrative.
- Write simply, clearly and in a consistent tone, preferably something informal or even conversational.
- Pay attention to searchability (see below).

The majority of blogs are stand-alone efforts but there are media organisations that collect, or aggregate, a suite of blogs under their banner: Gawker Media is the classic example here – founded in 2002, it incorporates sites such as Gizmodo (tech), Jezebel (feminism) and Lifehack (er, life hacks[18]). A more recent variation on this can be found in *Medium.com*, launched in 2012 to be 'a distraction free interface for writing' – *Medium*'s founders include Evan Williams, who also had a hand in setting up Blogger and Twitter. In effect, *Medium* provides a branded wrapper for writers: you sign on, write and it's published under the banner. The advantages are that your work is in the company of some distinguished writers, *Medium* as a whole probably has a wider reach than your individual blog (though your piece might get lost) and it looks great. Interestingly, *Medium* also gives each piece an estimated reading time, so people know what they are committing to.

Search Engine Optimisation

Search Engine Optimisation (SEO) is simply a way of ensuring that work you have published on the web can be found quickly by people looking for material on a particular topic or containing specific information. SEO is a technique to assist search engines like Google to deliver a useful result to their clients.

Google's advice on search engine optimisation is pretty straightforward – keep it simple and accurate if you want your copy to be found by both the web crawlers and those searching:

- Start by putting yourself in the shoes of someone looking for content like yours – what words or phrases would they type into the search engine?
- Build up from single words into likely phrases and complete questions.
- Incorporate those words and phrases into your headline and intro (and the sell/standfirst if you have one).
- Don't force keywords in unnaturally and don't cram in too many – the quality and flow of writing are important.

Google and other search engines change their algorithms from time to time, partly to make them more effective and partly to dissuade individuals and organisations from boosting their websites up the list of search results by gaming the system. It is difficult to get specific advice from the search engines on how to maximise SEO and it is probably more productive to think about providing useful, well-written content that does not hide its subject matter behind clever puns and delayed-drop intros.

Notes

1 Available online at http://bit.ly/harpersub (accessed 14 November 2014).
2 Available online at http://bit.ly/baxtersub (accessed 14 November 2014).
3 Available online at http://bit.ly/guardlosses (accessed 27 July 2015).
4 Available online at http://bit.ly/guardjobs (accessed 27 July 2015).
5 Available online at http://bit.ly/jenkins01 (accessed 15 November 2015).
6 Available online at http://bit.ly/goldhaber (accessed 15 November 2015).
7 Available online at http://bit.ly/coates01 (accessed 28 July 2015).
8 Available online at http://bit.ly/coates02 (accessed 15 November 2015).
9 Available online at http://bit.ly/bennett01 (accessed 28 July 2015).
10 Available online at https://about.twitter.com/company (accessed 28 July 2015).
11 Available online at http://bit.ly/faceuse (accessed 30 July 2015).
12 Available online at https://instagram.com/press/ (accessed 29 May 2015).
13 Available online at http://bit.ly/pinuse (accessed 29 July 2015).
14 Available online at https://instagram.com/p/5PBt-HzY5W/ (accessed 15 November 2015).
15 For advice on writing headlines and captions see *Subediting & Production for Journalists*.
16 Available online at http://bit.ly/instacaps (accessed 30 July 2015).
17 See also Chapter 4, 'Writing columns and blogs', page 91.
18 Available online at http://bit.ly/lihack (accessed 15 November 2015).

7
Writing for digital publication – longform

Jane Bentley

My inbox pinged today with a link to an article from the novelist Margaret Atwood entitled *It's Not Climate Change, It's Everything Change*, an expansive essay[1] which imagines a point in the future where we have no oil. In a second a simple click pushes me through to the website for the full article, where I see that 27 minutes is the stated reading time and that, to date, over 1,000 people have favourited it.

I settle in for the half-hour read and at the end am rewarded with more suggestions for similar pieces of 'Cli-Fi' – themed features on climate change – which the website has specially commissioned and collected.

I can bookmark, email and share the story via social media. I can comment on it above and below the fold. And in less time than it takes to walk to my newsagent I have gone through a gateway into a whole new genre of deep reporting or 'narrative journalism' that these days comes under the catch-all 'longform'.

Atwood's article was the subject of a regular e-newsletter drop by longform tech and science website *Matter*, sending through clickable headlines and story 'sells' that offer just enough content to pique your interest. The e-newsletter offers a seductive dose of long reads and non-fiction that comes straight to me, I don't have to go looking for it, and this helpfully illustrates the renaissance of longform journalism, in all its forms, online.

This chapter on writing for digital publication is dedicated to longform and its place in online journalism today. It will look at some of the popular players, from digital titans to streetwise start-ups, talk to some of the creators behind the content and also consider some of the challenges of funding this content.

Feature writing: full circle

When Pulitzer prizes were established in 1917 celebrating the original, investigative, emotional and untold stories published in the mainstream American press, the narrative feature form spanning anywhere from 2,000 to 12,000-plus words became a byword for quality. Deeply reported stories require 'deep pockets' noted Dan Gillmor (author of *We the Media*)[2] and the major press players and literary publishers were happy to fund them.

Later, particularly in the 1980s, magazine features developed alongside the technology; new desktop publishing software, in the form of QuarkXPress and Adobe InDesign, enabled magazine design and layout to take on increasingly creative forms, elevating the feature from straight prose to a multitude of formats that provided 'funny, sexy, and useful' content for its readers.[3]

This injection of page craft in the early 1990s led to exciting flatplanning by editors on the magazine newsstands particularly, leaving newspapers – with their column inches and typography bland by comparison – trailing in their wake. But just when journalists thought they'd mastered the art of creative story-telling in print, the internet came along and, well, you know the rest.

The rules of engagement

'Disruption' has been the favoured term used to describe the upheaval traditional newsrooms have experienced in the last 20 years. That young-gun the internet swept into town and started blowing away the cowboys and sheriffs who had swaggered around for decades, pretty much unchallenged.

Suddenly the new rules of writing were all about compression: delivering the 'maximum message in the minimum of phrase', even in individual characters. All of this you will have already gathered in the previous chapter, so I won't labour the point. But it's safe to say that features or 'long reads' as a form sort of sat on the shelf while we all tried to figure out what kinds of journalism worked best in this new screen-centric format.

Fast forward to the early noughties and the dust started to settle. A backlash of sorts against the churnalism and shovelware being put out by news organisations saw audiences searching for something altogether more wholesome and satisfying.

The *Guardian* feature writer Jon Henley points out that at this time there was also a determined reaction by some against the immediacy and short-attention-span-journalism that digital was driving us into. 'Influential people were saying, "We mustn't lose this tradition of what we traditionally call magazine features",' he says. A tradition that the USA has typically excelled in, with titles like the *New Yorker*, the *Atlantic*, *Esquire* and the *New York Times*. These publications set the benchmark for a lot of what we recognise as 'proper' longform today – deep reporting that is observational, emotional, informative and with something to say.

Definitions of the term are broad, however, and 'longform' is widely applied to feature stories of 800 words, all the way up to an 'e-book short' length of typically 12–15,000 words, and even up to a novel, plus essays (such as Atwood's) and profiles. For Henley there is a clear distinction, though. 'Longform is different to essays as it's about reporting,' he says. A useful point of view to discuss with editors of any publications you may be hoping to write for.

In the most recent decade the advent of shareability and analytics begat the rise of quality content as opposed to plain 'quick' content. Discerning readers spread the good stuff, whether it was a listicle or a longform article, and so the long-tail effect became common parlance.

Originally a phrase coined by *Wired* editor-in-chief Chris Anderson in 2004, the 'long-tail' effect is neatly defined by journalism.co.uk as:

> The effect of publishing content online and keeping it available in an archive. Unlike in a newspaper, old stories will continue to receive traffic long after publication date, hence the long tail.

Anderson wrote a book of the same name and US media executive Bob Benz noted afterwards:

> Anderson says a critical component of the long tail is and will be recommendations. People will act on recommendations from blogs, their friends and peers and, if we do our jobs, the media.[4]

Recognising this trend, Silicon Valley pioneers from Blogger and Twitter, among others, realised that open-source, easy-to-use content management systems and collaborative potential for text, combined perfectly with original, compelling storytelling. So they created new web-specific platforms and aggregators such as *The Atavist*, *Medium*, *Narrative.ly*, *Longreads* and *Longform* for feature stories, which are now largely celebrated as bespoke vehicles for longform writing.

Matter (owned by *Medium*) claims to craft 'hard-hitting narratives about big ideas', like the Cli-Fi collection as mentioned earlier, while *Longreads* is 'dedicated to helping people find and share the best storytelling in the world'. 'People get excited when they've read something that really moves them, and they want to be that story's biggest cheerleader,' *Longreads* founder Mark Armstrong told *Poynter.org* in 2012,[5] confirming the power of recommendations which in turn feeds the long tail.

In this vein the longform specialists illustrated above have created a fanbase, or community of readers, who join up as members in order to contribute to the stories with additional content, feedback or comments. The advocates help to spread the stories around the internet, ensuring that stories find their audiences and that willing readers who sign up for updates are also regularly offered original, interesting articles that the mainstream media diet doesn't necessarily provide.

WHAT I KNOW ABOUT LONGFORM: JON HENLEY – *GUARDIAN* INTERACTIVE FEATURES

What does longform mean to you?

I like the term longform, it makes a clear distinction between crafted and thoroughly reported longer pieces against an instant-snap news bite.

Key ingredients

Good story criteria still apply, so a story has to be important to its readership. The subject matter doesn't matter so much, it's more a different approach of tone. The main thing is that it has to be consistently interesting and *you* have to make it this way, by engaging your reader at every point that you can.

Behind the curtain

My conception of reporting is really very simple: you go somewhere interesting or unusual, you meet some people who are interesting or unusual, and you write about them in a way that is interesting and unusual. Longform for me satisfies those fundamental requirements.

What rules do you apply?

You need to address the head and the heart all the time. And your story has to have weight – there's got to be a density of real observed life. Plus you need a revealing line.

Think format

Everyone is still struggling with this, no one has yet worked out how to do it absolutely right for the screen. *Snowfall*'s integration of text and multimedia was beautifully done. It's essentially a *New Yorker*-length essay enlivened for a digital audience. But 17,000 words was a very big ask for people to read on screen.

Firestorm was 4,000–5,000 words but they used a lot of video. It had a gripping human family (characters, drama and human interest), we met them all in person, it had the weight of observed detail, and through that we were able to show a really important backstory – the effect of climate change on Australia. Showing a story in an unusual way, whatever the medium, this has to be the approach.

Longform needn't be 'exclusively text', some elements might be better told as a graphic or video – they might be more powerful.

Can anyone do it?

In principle everybody can if you approach it in the right spirit and abide by the rules. Some journalists are great reporters, some are great writers, really good longform requires you to do both.

In news writing you're always looking for a substantiating quote. What you're looking for in feature writing is a different type of component: a revealing or telling piece of dialogue or information, and you're building pictures of people and places.

Who inspires you?

Aggregators *Longform.org* and *Longreads.com*, and the *New Yorker*.

Where do you read these stories?

On my laptop at home or on my iPad or Kindle. I use Evernote *a lot* and the web browser extension Send to Kindle. I don't buy much paper these days.

What's the future for longform?

The hope is that huge, months-long projects will become a much slicker and quicker process. The ideal would be to tackle a breaking news story as a full interactive multimedia article in the future.

In the space of time that you used to have a big news text story for an old-fashioned first edition deadline, you would have a proper multimedia piece.

The confusing world of word counts

While the digital space doesn't necessarily put a limit on stories in the way that a printed page does, a good editor will still trim the fat, and each news organisation or website has its own set of working practices and guidelines. The following examples are benchmarks to consider, though there are many others out there you should look at – see useful links at the end of the chapter.

800+ words: lightweight

So where does longform begin? The word count threshold suggested here is 800, based on a typical feature length carried over from print publishing days but also supported by business website *Quartz*[6] which recommends you ditch 'medium length' articles altogether.

'Too much reporting is 700-word articles that everyone else has got,' says its editor-in-chief, Kevin Delaney.[7] Instead, this digitally native business news site takes a two-pronged content approach: focusing on short, shareable posts under 500 words and long in-depth features of 800 words and over.

Its research, Delaney told a conference in 2013, shows that articles of between 500 and 800 words are too long to be shareable, and too short to be in-depth. 'People read short, fast content on the web,' he said, 'and also longform, analytical pieces.'[8]

In a physical sense some of its longer pieces are straight prose, but some make good use of charts and infographics for its knowledge-hungry readers. This brings us on to formats again, or how a feature can appear, but we will return to this discussion later on in the chapter.

1,000+ words: midweight

This middleweight category is heavily populated with work from major news organisations as well as many of the longform web outlets mentioned previously. Not always tagged as longform or long reads, you may well find 'features' of this length that still qualify as in-depth reporting.

Authors can range from expert journalists with familiar and trusted bylines, to bloggers, specialists in particular fields (health, tech, cycling etc) as well as citizen journalists. The barriers to entry of traditional or mainstream news outlets are often removed with some of the native web platforms, and the

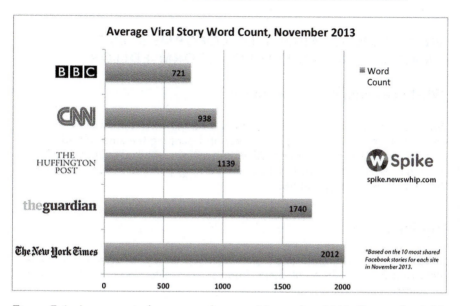

Figure 7.1 Average viral story word count, November 2013. Copyright @ blog. newswhip.com.

communities there regulate the quality through collaboration on stories largely successfully.

NewsWhip's figures for the average length of the ten most shared stories from some of the biggest publishers, including the BBC, CNN, the *Huffington Post*, the *Guardian* and the *New York Times*, ranged from 721 (BBC) up to 2,012 (NYT) (see Figure 7.1).

Medium published statistics that claim the ideal story post length is seven minutes long, or seven minutes of reading time, which equates to about 1,600 words of text (less for picture-heavy or 'rich media' stories). 'This doesn't mean we should all start forcing our posts to be seven minutes! There is enormous variance. Great posts perform well regardless of length, and bad posts certainly don't get better when you stretch them out.'[9]

See Buzzfeed www.buzzfeed.com/bigstories
See Huffington Post www.huffingtonpost.com/news/longreads

WHAT I KNOW ABOUT LONGFORM: STEVE KANDELL – *BUZZFEED* LONGFORM EDITOR

What does longform mean to you?

We're of the mind that 'longform' isn't really a thing – that term was essentially invented a couple of years ago as a way of describing the kind of traditional deeply reported and carefully edited writing that the web had supposedly risen up to destroy; people focus too much on the 'long' part and not enough on the 'form' part. We just do features.

Key ingredients

It has to be something no one's read before. There's just too much to compete with for your time out there, from our own site alone, much less the rest of the internet.

If it's a profile of someone familiar, it better have something in it you didn't know about before. If it's a true crime story, or a dive into some cultural trend or phenomenon, there has to be some idea or condition that this is revealing.

What rules do you apply?

Our stories are definitely worked on at a slower pace than most stories in our newsroom, but we have all the autonomy and freedom we could ever hope for. We're very lucky.

What successes has Buzzfeed had?

No one really knew whether our longer stories would be read and shared the way other things on the site had been. We're so lucky that we are doing this at a place where there's at least an opportunity for people to find our stories; but from there, the stories themselves have to do the work.

But the one thing I don't think people are worried about is whether or not people have the interest in or capacity to read carefully crafted 7,000-word stories on a glowing screen. Sure they will, as long as the words are good.

What *hasn't* worked so well?

I think we've seen some types of stories that are mainstays of certain types of traditional magazine feature wells not quite translate to the social web.

Celebrity profiles, war stories – these just aren't really things people share, and the impulse to want to show someone else what you've just read, whether it's an accurate metric or not, still feels like a pretty admirable goal. These are things we learn all the time, and the lessons change quickly.

One thing we don't do a lot of is heavily produced multimedia layouts. We think a lot about design, especially opening images, but past that, our time and energy go into the story.

Who inspires you?

The *New Yorker* and *New York Times Magazine* are still, on any given week, likely to put out multiple stories that we're in awe of.

But the thing about right now is that any story can come from anywhere and still get everyone's attention if it's good enough. The playing field is largely levelled: if you're doing something that's really exciting, really exemplary quality, it has a chance to be seen in ways that things like newsstand distribution would have never allowed.

What's the future for longform?

Feature writing has always been about finding a good idea, thinking about the idea, pitching the idea, reporting the idea, writing a draft, writing four more drafts, then writing another draft. This has existed forever and it should continue to, regardless of the means in which that story gets delivered to your eyeballs.

What we do is so conventional, we're just very fortunate that we do it at another place that has innovated in other ways so that we can afford this luxury. Which isn't to say that there isn't a lot that can be done in terms of presentation and distribution, but the *writing* – I hope that doesn't develop at all.

3,000+ words: heavyweight

At the meatier end of the spectrum the *New Yorker*, the *Sunday Times*, the *Atlantic* and the *Guardian* employ legendary contributors on speed dial and the healthy budgets required to deliver longform craft. Names like John McPhee, George Packer, James Meek, John Lanchester and Andrew O'Hagan are heroes for Jon Henley, who worked on the *Guardian*'s rich multimedia feature *Firestorm* and has written longreads covering (eg) the Greek euro crisis and the future for British milk.

This is a 'muscular' form of feature reporting according to Jon. And it's no coincidence that he frequently references the weight of information in relation to writing technique:

> The difference in tone with longform compared to other features or articles is the weight of reported detail, having strong characters, transmitting and evoking emotion. The very best longform pieces strike a delicate and brilliant balance between the two poles of a story: the emotional register and the informational register. So you have news and colour in one hand and emotion and information in the other.

For those aspiring to develop their own writing style along these lines, the building blocks of great feature craft still apply. Editors, writers and academic practitioners all hark back to Hemingway's mantra of less telling, more showing. 'Features are all about showing,' Jon says, 'showing people, places, observations.'

The *Guardian's* online longreads are typically between 3,000 and 5,000 words. They appear three times a week in a dedicated two-page slot in the paper and on the website. This section was established in 2014, according to the *Guardian*, to 'showcase a wide range of in-depth analysis and essays, as well as detailed profile pieces and on-the-ground reportage. . . . The pieces will cover politics, both domestic and international, culture, science, technology and everything in between.'[10]

This level of reporting is 'undeniably expensive,' says Jon, 'often requiring foreign travel, a week or more of reporting.' And the time required to deliver a story of this length can be considerable, from a couple of weeks to months, even years: a rare luxury in today's hard-pressed newsrooms.

But Jon and his *Guardian* colleagues maintain that this kind of journalism needs to be a part of any self-respecting universal news organisation offering. And a recent appointment of a former *New Yorker* editor from the US to their longreads department has brought a new approach that Jon describes as 'very American'.

This means that a feature is filed as a draft, going through two, three or even four drafts before getting to the final product. This protracted development gradually builds up the article to ensure that all areas are as 'weighty' as they possibly can be. From the writer's perspective this may mean 'days of writing and rewriting'. But for off-diary pieces, argues Jon, the results speak for themselves – and their engagement figures prove it.

So while this approach means slower, costly editorial that doesn't automatically deliver the hits online in a way news can, the trade-off is that the long-tail effect means readers often discover the story much later, it can have a second or third 'life', and the engagement rate is substantially increased. Jon says that the average length of reading time for their *Firestorm* article was 17.5 minutes, when the biggest figure for a *Guardian* article before that had been just four.

For a closer look at some of the stages involved with a major feature process, from idea genesis to finished article, take a look at the blog of *Wired* magazine's editor-in-chief Scott Dadich[11] who documented a real-time behind-the-scenes account of their cover story on film director Charlie Kaufman.

See *Guardian* Longreads: www.theguardian.com/news/series/the-long-read
See *The Battle for the Soul of British Milk* (*Guardian*): http://bit.ly/1E3JPWk
See *The Sunday Times's* Fifa Files Insight Team investigations (paywall): http://
    thetim.es/1p968EF

A familiar (inter)face

The renaissance of longform also owes something to the way we now experience articles online. While everyone is still experimenting and figuring things out in this area, screen data enable developers and publishers to understand reader behaviour better, and content management systems are improving all the time.

The elements driving these improvements include:

- **Responsive design** – so stories read well on multiple platforms, from laptops to smartphones to tablets.
- **Simplified content management systems** – familiar CMS iterations that are open source, widely available, and even sometimes offer template formats for creating multimedia articles.
- **Parallax scrolling** – fluid scrolling that creates an illusion of depth with text overlaid on pictures or multimedia. This trend offers a simplified, widescreen, more-book-chapter-like reading experience where text is typically centred in a wide column and in an enlarged font size. Often enhanced with rich multimedia features such as photography, illustrations, audio or video.
- **Proliferation of mobile devices** – globally there are 3 billion internet users in 2015[12] and 42% of the world have access to the web. Audiences and readers are global now rather than purely regional.
- **Analytics** – instead of waiting for readers to write a letter to tell you how much they disliked or enjoyed an article, each element of a story is measurable; from the number of referrals, recommendations and likes it gets; to the amount of shares – and with whom and from where in the world; the actual time spent reading content; A/B testing headlines to see which styles are more successful. . . . This is all part of the journalist's working environment today.

So while technology is very much part of the picture, it isn't directing the content. Journalists and publishers are investing heavily in new software and working in tandem with developer teams to create the platforms, tools and styles that enable them to tell the stories they want to tell in the best ways possible.

This journalist–developer relationship is another more recent change to newsroom practice. Previously web development was a job for external, third-party businesses, but just as writers work closely with editors, subs and designers, developers are now a part of many teams.

There is still some scepticism about the viability of a hand-in-hand relationship, but there are organisations out there making it work – the BBC, *Vox*, *Financial Times* and *Guardian* among them. Richard Sambrook, former director of BBC News and now professor of journalism at Cardiff University, says that these news organisations 'need technologists who understand journalism, and journalists who understand technology'.[13]

Rachel Bartlett is a former *Journalism.co.uk* senior reporter who now works as editorial and planning manager for *Shorthand.com*, a platform designed to make text, images and multimedia packages engaging and 'immersive', while also offering a simple CMS interface for people to upload their content to. *Shorthand* has worked with companies such as the BBC, the *Mirror* and *Elle* magazine:

> With the rise of mobile traffic, there has been a move to responsive design online by many media organisations in recent years, which means experiences are not only beautiful on desktop screens, but across smaller devices too.
>
> The rise of parallax scrolling and the ability for storytellers to use that to add depth and layers to their narratives, as well as the ongoing development of easy-to-use tools for creating embeddable, interactive media, also means online storytellers can again think differently about how they can best tell part of a story.

The user interface, or UI, might not be the first thing that comes to mind when you think about longform writing online, but these developments impact *usability* (navigation and how well the story scrolls for example), *readability* (text size, page furniture) and *shareability* (how easy it is to favourite the article, share via social media channels, email or bookmark the article). Good UI today includes responsive design that is multi-platform and multi-device friendly.

On *Medium.com*, which also owns *Matter*, you sign up as an author and can start writing and sharing your stories straight away. '*Medium* is not about who you are or whom you know, but about what you have to say,' says the site. They have removed as many technical barriers as possible for writers so that they can focus on the words.

It explains its simple functionality as follows:

1.   Simple and beautiful UI is responsive.
2.   Collaborative principle enables peer input before you publish a piece.
3.   Its algorithms help you find your audience regardless of your name, status and topic.

The benefit of this for the readers is (mostly) comfortable and seamless screen reading, whatever device people happen to be reading your stories on, which helps contribute to that magic metric: engagement. 'If a reader is spending 25 minutes with something your publication has created, that's ultimately a very good thing,' *Longreads*' Mark Armstrong says.

How readers find your work has been touched on in the previous chapter. But one example in the longform space worth mentioning is Shorthand Social – a new version of Shorthand Immersive that helps users better promote their work within their existing network[14] by *automatically* generating tweets from content.

With Social, 'users can now sign in with Twitter before using Shorthand to create media-rich stories, in a similar manner to *Medium*,' Alistair Reid says. 'This notion of the "intelligent story", which now helps users better promote their work within their existing network, is the first step in a process which [they hope] will help empower freelancers around the world.'

Let's return to that screen experience: the physical format of a feature on the printed page has been carefully conceived and crafted so that every element of it is readable, communicative and has impact whether with text or images. On-screen, the same rules apply, though a more pared-down treatment appears to work best with a responsive UI. In this way, textual feature craft such as pull (or blown) quotes, captions, subheads and fact boxes add detail and subtly help you navigate through the thousands of words contained in the main narrative.

'The web is a visual medium,' *Quartz*'s Kevin Delaney says, and so illustrative charts and infographics can also add to the storytelling as mentioned previously.

The next level of page craft takes advantage of these more advanced UIs by including multimedia elements such as video, audio, mapping, slideshows and more. It's here where the truly 'immersive' or interactive longform has been blazing trails and picking up Pulitzers. And the next section is entirely devoted to this rich media storytelling.

See Shorthand Pro, Shorthand Immersive and Shorthand Social: www. shorthand.com
See Wordpress plug-in Aesop Story Engine: http://aesopstoryengine.com/
See Racontr: https://racontr.com/

WHAT I KNOW ABOUT LONGFORM: RACHEL BARTLETT – *SHORTHAND* EDITORIAL PLANNING

What does longform mean to you?

It simply suggests a narrative which isn't a snapshot of something. But it's also moved away from being strictly linked with long verses of text. While many outlets still do deliver largely text-focused, long-form narratives, that are still engaging and powerful to read, there are also other examples of 'longform' experiences that have less reliance on text to lead the narrative.

Think of more photo-essay style pieces – they're still offering a deep level of engagement, just in a visuals-driven way.

Behind the curtain

Arguably, digital should take away any ideas of specific lengths to fill on a page, and let the story remain at the heart of what is the best treatment. But that also means there can be the temptation of an 'endless' space and therefore the need for strict editorial oversight remains.

Think format

What I love to see are immersive experiences that really serve to better tell a story, not just in terms of how the narrative is communicated in text and image, but where each visual, each piece of interactivity or each transition, adds something not just to the experience, but to the reader's understanding of the content, the meaning of the message, the atmosphere of the scene.

Who inspires you?

Great places to look of course include the big media organisations like the *BBC*, the *Guardian*, *New York Times*, *Wired* – although many smaller, regional outlets are also working hard to innovate in this space.

And it's not just the realm of news organisations. We've worked with a number of NGOs, charities, museums – all with fantastic, deep-dive narratives to share, and keen to do so in a way that will bring the content to life.

What impact has *Shorthand* had?

I see a lot of excitement about the opportunities that this form of storytelling is giving journalists and other content creators. In some cases, it gives them the ability to be more expressive in their work, more creative as they perhaps go beyond the boundaries of their CMS.

From a workflow perspective, many find it's important to have a discussion in the very early stages about what treatment might be best for this story, and considering if it would be better explored in a certain way.

Developments like this also highlight the importance, and tremendous value, of having solid analytics tracking, to ensure that content creators understand the best strategy for their content, and their audience. When trying new things it's great to experiment, but it's even better to learn.

What's the future for longform?

It's always difficult to try and identify what the future looks like in an industry that has changed so significantly in recent years. But certainly in the near future I expect to see even greater integration of interactivity as part of the storytelling, putting more control in the reader's hands as they navigate through the narrative, and generally more confidence and experimentation with visually driven storytelling.

What isn't going to change is the fact that the story remains key – and so the focus should be on delivering a strong story, that is well told (in whatever media format). That's what any reader wants today, and tomorrow.

The new normal

When John Branch's 17,000-word feature for the *New York Times* called *Snowfall: The Avalanche at Tunnel Creek* won the 2013 Pulitzer prize for feature writing, a new seam in multimedia or 'rich media' longform cracked wide open.

A weighty, emotional narrative that told the stories of 16 skiers and snowboarders tragically caught up in an avalanche in Washington, USA, it blended sounds and visuals of snow blowing across incredible landscapes and embedded videos and slideshows of those involved. The design team created moving infographics that mapped out the terrain, geography and journey of the avalanche, so that no detail was left untouched.

Read it and you'll discover a brilliant example of classic longform writing craft (from a writer who had been shortlisted by Pulitzer previously for feature writing) that also balances multimedia so that it carefully adds to the storytelling at key points. It garnered more than 3.4 million page views and 2.9 million visitors, crucially bringing in new readers to the *NYT* for the first time.

Described as 'beautiful', and lauded as 'the *New York Times* wins the internet', it even became a verb in newsrooms: 'Can we snowfall this story?'

It has also had its critics, who decry the 'off-putting' multimedia and the fact it wasn't mobile friendly – a useful reminder that just because you can, doesn't necessarily mean you should, and that the needs of your audience are paramount.

Today, interactive longform is arguably the new normal. Mequoda CEO Don Nicholas says: 'Modern day multi-platform journalism means journalists are expected to do a lot more than report the news' – and it is this practice and mindset change that is driving journalism forward at pace.

Of course the basics still apply: you're just expected to do a lot more, smarter and faster, and also be prepared to experiment, fail and learn as you go. If you're only as good as your next story, then your next story could well be a very different treatment or even on a different platform from the one you used last week. Keep up!

In terms of interactive or immersive storytelling you need to consider – if not be personally expert at – high-quality visuals, audio, video, other story devices, page craft and dramatic story structure. The major news organisations have teams of professionals who collectively plan and execute each of these packages very closely and carefully. The Wordpress plug-in Aesop borrows the aesthetic established by the big players, but is used more often by individuals at much smaller specialist or independent publications, who research, source, shoot, edit, write, upload and publish each and every bit of the story themselves.

This multi-skilled version of a journalist today is very broad. Institutions such as universities, accrediting bodies and news organisations are offering increasing multimedia training that brings in video, audio, photography, data and analytics, social media, coding, entrepreneurialism and more alongside the traditional basics of good journalism.

One of the main skills building up to more enhanced story versions is: what is best to add or include and how to treat it? Jon Henley's advice: 'Exploit the idea of choosing the right medium for each part of your message – that's what multimedia longform work is about.'

See *Snowfall* (*New York Times*): http://nyti.ms/1dQ0jHo
See *Firestorm* (*Guardian*): http://bit.ly/1bix0J3
See *A Game of Shark and Minnow* (*New York Times*): http://nyti.ms/1cV4ih3
See *In the Belly of the Beast* (*Rolling Stone*): http://rol.st/ID5xs3
See *A Week in the Mysterious Sleeping Villages of Kazakhstan* (Buzzfeed): http://bzfd.it/1fSvfJm

Do it yourself

If, after reading this, you have an overwhelmingly positive view of the longform space, then you can be confident that there are still guardians of the craft experimenting in new ways on both 'old' and new publishing platforms. One of the challenges ahead exists around effective and innovative distribution models. *Contributoria.com*, for instance, was an open, collaborative, crowd-funded website, launched in 2014. Community members could suggest topics to be written about and donate cash, and journalists pitched for those stories and got paid to write them. The site reached beyond pure media, with charities and NGOs also involved, and had writers based all over the world; it closed in September 2015 after 21 issues.

Through the Cracks: Crowdfunding in Journalism (http://throughcracks.com) is a useful website reporting on innovative journalism forms that use crowd-sourcing as a revenue stream. The former editor of Contributoria, Sarah Hartley, said: 'The closure of Contributoria shouldn't reflect any particular trend in crowdfunding for journalism. People clearly want to be part of the journalism process, and the team here feels crowdfunding will continue to be a big opportunity in the future. If anything, Contributoria merely scratched the surface.'[15]

Another challenge is execution, or design. Many of the current CMSes are templated, which reduces the barriers for users or writers, but this has led some critics to say the digital experience feels very samey. Once you've followed the recommended links contained in this chapter, you will no doubt make up your own mind about that.

But there's no denying that the democratisation of the internet is also a force for good in this area. The news media name-checked frequently here maintain their professional status as storytellers, reporters and innovators. But also new homes for longform mean that stories that 'aren't subject to the editorial agenda'[16] can find their audience too. As *Medium* says: 'Our collective, casual, everyday shares demonstrate that millions of people have the power of a printing press at their fingertips. (And they use it.) That is an amazing advancement.'

Notes

1   Available online at https://medium.com/matter/it-s-not-climate-change-it-s-everything-change-8fd9aa671804 – Margaret Atwood, *Matter*.
2   Available online at http://archive.wired.com/wired/archive/13.09/start.html?pg=2 – Dan Gillmor, *We the Media*.
3   Mary Hogarth, *How To Launch A Magazine In This Digital Age*.

4   Available online at www.opposable-thumbs.com/2005/02/13/my-those-blogos pherians-have-a-long-tail/ – Bob Benz, My Those Blogospherians Have a Long Tail.

5   Available online at www.poynter.org/news/mediawire/190421/as-longform-finds-a-new-home-at-buzzfeed-perhaps-its-a-good-gateway-drug/ – Caitlin Johnston, Poynter.org.

6   Available online at www.qz.com.

7   Available online at https://www.journalism.co.uk/news/-smartden-why-quartz-does-not-publish-500-to-800-word-articles/s2/a554444/ – Sarah Marshall, Journalism. co.uk.

8   Ibid.

9   Available online at https://medium.com/data-lab/the-optimal-post-is-7-minutes-74b9f41509b – Medium's Data-lab, Medium.com.

10 Available online at www.theguardian.com/gnm-press-office/2014/sep/12/guardian-newspaper-to-showcase-new-look-and-brand-new-journal-section (accessed 15 November 2015).

11 Available online at www.wired.com/category/storyboard/ – Scott Dadich, Wired blog.

12 Available online at www.mobileindustryreview.com/2015/01/3-billion-internet-users-2015.html – Roland Banks, Mobile Industry Review.

13 Available online at www.theguardian.com/media/2014/apr/27/journalists-coders-creative-future – Richard Sambrook, Guardian.

14 Available online at https://www.journalism.co.uk/news/new-shorthand-social-to-help-writers-promote-their-work/s2/a565099/ – Alistair Reid, Journalism.co.uk.

15 Available online at http://throughcracks.com/contributoria-shuts-down-crowd funding/ (accessed 17 November 2015).

16 Available online at https://www.journalism.co.uk/news/contributoria-launches-topics-to-allow-the-public-to-commission-stories/s2/a564337/ – Abigail Edge, Journalism.co.uk.

Further reading

The Best American Magazine Writing 2014 (plus previous years), Columbia University Press

Vice's longform archive www.vice.com/en_uk/tag/longform

James Bennet, Editor in chief, The Atlantic www.theatlantic.com/business/archive/ 2013/12/against-long-form-journalism/282256/

Useful links

Narrative.ly http://narrative.ly/ – New York 'Local stories, deeply told'

The Atavist https://www.atavist.com/ – New York 'Where stories begin'

Longform http://longform.org/feed.rss – New York 'Great longform non-fiction, past and present, formatted for later reading'

Longreads http://longreads.com/ – USA *'Dedicated to helping people find and share the best storytelling in the world'*

Buzzfeed www.buzzfeed.com/tag/longreads – New York and London *'The social news and entertainment company'*

Delayed Gratification www.slow-journalism.com – London *'The last to breaking news'*

Quartz www.qz.com – New York *'We publish bracingly creative and intelligent journalism with a broad worldview'*

The Awl www.theawl.com – New York *'Be less stupid'*

London Review of Books www.lrb.co.uk – London *'Standing up for the tradition of the literary and intellectual essay in English'*

The Riveter www.therivetermagazine.com – Minneapolis *'Riveting storytelling by Women'*

8
Style

Murder your darlings

The traditional view on English style is simply put. Be clear; avoid ornament; let the message reveal itself. From Samuel Johnson and Jonathan Swift in the eighteenth century to George Orwell in the twentieth and Elmore Leonard in the twenty-first, writers and literary critics have agreed. Style is not something to be strained for or added on: it is there in the writer – or the subject – waiting to be expressed. What is needed is plainness, decorum, economy, precision – above all, clarity. What is not needed is rhetoric or embellishment.

Quoting a college tutor, Dr Johnson pronounced: 'Read over your compositions, and where ever you meet with a passage which you think is particularly fine, strike it out.' And echoing Dr Johnson, Sir Arthur Quiller-Couch told Cambridge undergraduates in 1913: 'Whenever you feel an impulse to perpetrate a piece of exceptionally fine writing, obey it – whole-heartedly – and delete it before sending your manuscript to press. *Murder your darlings.*'

As his Oxford opposite number, J Middleton Murry, noted a few years later, 'These *obiter dicta* of the masters . . . all point the same way; they all lay stress solely on the immediate nature of style; they all reduce the element of art or artifice to nothingness.'

A famous campaigner for simple English, Sir Ernest Gowers, wrote an influential book intended to help civil servants in their use of written English – he called it *Plain Words*. It is full of passages like

> The most prevalent disease in present-day writing is a tendency to say what one has to say in as complicated a way as possible. Instead of being simple, terse and direct, it is stilted, long-winded and circumlocutory; instead of choosing the simple word it prefers the unusual; instead of the plain phrase, the cliché.

In the United States the traditional message has been exactly the same. William Strunk, whose book *The Elements of Style* was later revised by E B White, wrote in 1918:

> Young writers often suppose that style is a garnish for the meat of prose, a sauce by which a dull dish is made palatable. Style has no such separate entity; it is non-detachable, unfilterable. . . . The approach to style is by way of plainness, simplicity, orderliness, sincerity.

More recently, in a piece published in the *New York Times*, the crime writer Elmore Leonard issued his own rules of good writing, such as: 'Never use a verb other than "said" to carry dialogue', 'Never use an adverb to modify the verb "said"' and 'If it sounds like writing, I rewrite it.'

This emphasis on plainness and simplicity has been repeated by those who lay down the law about journalistic style. *The Economist Style Guide*, first published in the 1980s, quotes George Orwell's 'six elementary rules' from a famous essay, 'Politics and the English Language', written in 1946:

1 Never use a metaphor, simile or other figure of speech which you are used to seeing in print.
2 Never use a long word where a short word will do.
3 If it is possible to cut out a word, always cut it out.
4 Never use the passive where you can use the active.
5 Never use a foreign phrase, a scientific word or a jargon word if you can think of an everyday English equivalent.
6 Break any of these rules sooner than say anything outright barbarous.

The fog index

The Americans, who adopted journalism education and training before the British, developed a systematic way of measuring the readability of newspapers and magazines. The journalism trainer Robert Gunning gave his name in 1944 to the Gunning Fog Index, which sets out to show how clear or obscure ('foggy') writing is. The index is based on counting the long words and working out the length of an average sentence in a sample passage. A formula translates this into the approximate number of years of education needed to understand it. The higher the fog index, the harder the passage is to understand.

Thus a popular American TV magazine scores 6, equivalent to sixth grade or six years of education, while the *Ladies' Home Journal* scores 8, the *National Geographic* 10, and *Time* magazine 12 – equivalent to high school senior or 12 years of education.

Some British trainers apply the index to our media: a typical airport novel would score 6, a downmarket newspaper (the *Mirror*) 8–10, a middle-market paper (the *Express*) 10–12, an upmarket paper (the *Telegraph*) 12–14, a specialist periodical (*Pulse*) 14–16 – and the small print in an insurance company document 20. Whether or not you adopt the index, the idea that underlies it is essential: to write successfully for a publication you must write so that its readers understand you.

Write the way you talk

In the orthodox Anglo-American tradition there is a second commandment: that good writing should mirror speech rather than aspire to be something else, something artificial, contrived, self-consciously literary. As William Hazlitt put it in the early nineteenth century:

> To write a genuine familiar or true English style is to write as anyone would speak in common conversation, who had a thorough command and choice of words, or who could discourse with ease, force and perspicuity, setting aside all pedantic and oratorical flourishes.

Later, Cyril Connolly attacked what he called the mandarin style

> loved by literary pundits, by those who would make the written word as unlike as possible to the spoken one. It is the style of those writers whose tendency is to make their language convey more than they mean or more than they feel, it is the style of most artists and all humbugs.

Both Hazlitt and Connolly were journalists – and their message has been enthusiastically endorsed by later experts on journalistic style. Harold Evans in his classic *Newsman's English* (republished in 2000 as *Essential English for Journalists, Editors and Writers*) quotes Connolly with approval and recommends 'a clear, muscular and colloquial style'; Nicholas Bagnall in *Newspaper Language* quotes Hazlitt and calls his 'the best definition I know of the true language of journalism'.

In one of his ten principles of clear statement Robert Gunning takes the argument a stage further and urges 'Write the way you talk', while John Whale in his book *Put It in Writing* repeats the point in more formal British English – 'Write as you speak.'

For all sorts of reasons – including the powerful influence on print of TV and radio – this link between the spoken word and journalistic writing is now stronger than ever.

Metaphors are more fun

Both these ideas – write plainly and clearly; write as you speak – are obviously relevant to anyone learning journalism. The first is essential in basic news writing and instructional copy (telling readers how to mend a fuse, make an omelette, fill in a tax form). But that is not the end of the matter.

Unfortunately – in journalism as in writing generally – the rule is often assumed to apply across the board, whereas it does not. Good style cannot be reduced to the slogan 'Write plainly and clearly'.

As the American writer Richard Lanham points out in a little-known but forceful attack on the classics, *Style: An Anti-Textbook*: 'People seldom write simply to be clear. They have designs on their fellow men. Pure prose is as rare as pure virtue, and for the same reasons.'

Lanham ridicules The Books for preaching that the best style is the never noticed, for recommending that prose style should, like the state under Marxism, wither away, leaving the plain facts shining unto themselves. 'People, even literary people, seldom content themselves with being clear. They invent jargons, argot . . . and even when they succeed in being clear it is often only to seem clever.'

It is not easy to find examples of great writers who wrote 'plainly and clearly'. Certainly not the poets Chaucer, Shakespeare, Keats and Eliot; and not the novelists from Fielding to Martin Amis by way of Dickens and Lawrence. Even the literary preachers didn't always practise plainness. Dr Johnson was famously florid rather than plain; Swift, the scourge of looseness and incorrectness, often got carried away.

On the other hand, George Orwell, journalist, novelist, literary critic, is perhaps the best exponent of the plain style in English literature. His work is content-driven and in many ways he provides an excellent model of control, simplicity and precision.

Then of course there is Ernest Hemingway, master storyteller, Nobel prize-winner, another novelist who started as a journalist – his style is famous for its apparent simplicity. Here's a paragraph from his last great book, *The Old Man and the Sea*:

> The old man had seen many great fish. He had seen many that weighed more than a thousand pounds and he had caught two of that size in his life, but never alone. Now alone, and out of sight of land, he was fast to the biggest fish that he had ever seen and bigger than he had ever heard of, and his left hand was still as tight as the gripped claws of an eagle.

Note that word 'apparent' applied to 'simplicity': here is the use of deliberate repetition (for example, 'had seen many' repeated early on), the characteristic use of 'and' (three times in the last sentence), the gradual increase in sentence length, all contributing to a rich and powerful rhythm. The paragraph ends with the simile of the eagle's claws – which stands out from the 'plainness' of the rest.

Hemingway's prose then is not as simple as it looks. Other great writers of the twentieth century were dense (Faulkner), ornate (Nabokov) – or just plain difficult (Joyce).

As in literature so in personal life, politics, business, advertising – how can anybody argue that all speakers and writers aspire to clarity first and foremost? Of course, they have to be capable of clarity and know when to use it. But they don't use it all the time, not if they are arguing a case, wooing a woman or a man, playing a scene for laughs, showing off, selling a secondhand car . . .

Then there is the delight that so many speakers and writers take in playing with words. As Lanham puts it:

> People seldom content themselves with plain utterance even in daily life. It gets boring. . . . They prefer the metaphorical, the indirect expression to the straightforward, literal one. They are not trying to be literary. Metaphors are just more fun.

Clarity, clarity, clarity[1]

But there is a strong – indeed overwhelming – argument that, whatever politicians, lovers and secondhand car dealers may do, journalists must be clear above all; that journalism has no point otherwise; that an essential part of its function is to interrogate the politicians and conmen, to represent and communicate with the ordinary person confronted by authority, salesmanship, jargon, pretension and so on. Journalism must be clear.

Individual words and phrases must be clear so that your reader can understand them. For example, you must be careful with technical terms – a word suitable for a specialist periodical might be too abstruse for a daily paper. And, just as important, anything you write must be clear in structure: you must say things in the right order – without aimlessly repeating yourself or digressing too far from your main point.

Does this mean that the traditionalists are right after all? For journalism (as opposed to other kinds of writing) do we have to go back to the slogan 'Write plainly and clearly'?

---

1 This heading is a quotation from *The Elements of Style*: it is clear – but the rhetoric of repetition makes it far from plain.

Certainly, if journalism could be reduced to plainness and clarity, life would be much simpler and well-edited listings pages could stand as the perfect model of good style. But obviously this won't do. So we have to think again.

Plainness and clarity are associated for two reasons. First, to repeat the point, there are certain kinds of journalistic writing (basic news, instructional copy) where they belong together. Second, the easiest, safest way to achieve clarity is by plainness: avoid frills and you can be confident you will get your meaning across without having to strain too hard.

This is why trainee journalists are instructed to write plainly: to learn to walk before they start running. And this is why style manuals that concentrate on the basics tend to elaborate Orwell's 'six elementary rules' into the Ten Commandments of Plain Writing – each one to do with keeping it simple and cutting out clutter. (*English for Journalists*, which includes a chapter on style, takes this general approach.)

The point is not that these instructions are wrong but that they are incomplete: plainness is not all. For if we distinguish between plainness and clarity, we can see that journalism – though it must have clarity – should not necessarily be plain. It should be plain where plainness is a virtue – as in basic news and instructional copy – and it should be coloured where colour is called for.

A personal style

Feature writers, for example, often develop a strongly personal style – opinionated, anecdotal, gossipy. Columnists cannot do without one. They are celebrated – and paid – as much for their style as for their content. They are read because people enjoy their word play and tricks of style.

Here is A A Gill, who writes about restaurants and television for the *Sunday Times*:

> Can we just get the organic thing clear? Organic does not mean additive-free; it means some additives and not others. Organic does not mean your food hasn't been washed with chemicals, frozen or kept fresh with gas, or that it has not been flown around the world. Organic does not necessarily mean it is healthier, or will make you live longer; nor does it mean tastier, fresher, or in some way improved.
>
> Organically farmed fish is not necessarily better than wild fish. Organically reared animals didn't necessarily live a happier life than non-organic ones – and their death is no less traumatic.
>
> More importantly, organic does not mean that the people who picked, packed, sowed and slaughtered were treated fairly, paid properly, or were

free from artificial exploitation. The Chinese workers who drowned in Morecambe Bay were picking organic cockles for a pittance. If you really want to feed the hunger in your conscience, buy Fairtrade.

So what does organic actually mean? Buggered if I know. It usually means more expensive. Whatever the original good intentions of the organic movement, their good name has been hijacked by supermarkets, bijoux delicatessens and agri-processors as a value-added designer label. Organic comes with its own basket of aspiration, snobbery, vanity and fear that retailers on tight margins can exploit. And what I mind most about it is that it has reinvigorated the old class distinction in food. There is them that have chemical-rich, force-fed battery dinner and us that have decent, healthy, caring lunch. It is the belief that you can buy not only with a clear conscience, but a colon that works like the log flume at Alton Towers.

In general, I applaud and agree with many of the aims of environmentally careful producers, but it is time we all admitted that the label 'organic' has been polluted with cynicism, sentiment, sloppy practice and lies to the point where it is intellectually and practically bankrupt.

And it hasn't made anyone a better cook.
A A Gill, *Table Talk: Sweet and Sour, Salt and Bitter*, Orion, 2007

Reviewers are essentially people with opinions – the stronger the better. But a distinctive style is a great advantage because it can make a reviewer's view of the work easy to grasp and remember – as well as making the piece entertaining to read. If you read this kind of reviewer regularly, you get used to their attitudes and can more easily work out what you would think in their place.

Incidentally, there's no escaping the point that knocking review copy – like bad news – sells more papers than puffs do. Writers like Gill are often compulsive reading in their destruction of mediocre television. Programme producers may not like it – but most readers do.

Even news stories are sometimes written to tease, intrigue and entertain as well as to inform. And while instructional copy must remain plain and simple, the sections introducing it can be anything but.

Take cookery journalism, for example: recipes must be plain, step-by-step, no frills; but the writing that introduces the recipes is often evocative, atmospheric, allusive. Before readers get down to business in the kitchen, they want to be seduced by the scent of rosemary, the softness of raspberry, the crispness of celery, while all the time the Mediterranean murmurs in the background.

The new journalism

And the new journalism, meaning the adoption by mainly American journalists of various experimental techniques from the mid-1960s onwards, is the opposite of plain. For example, Tom Wolfe, pioneer and joint editor of the definitive anthology *The New Journalism*, explains his lavish use of dots, dashes, exclamation marks, italics and so on as essentially FUN:

> I found a great many pieces of punctuation and typography lying around dormant when I came along – and I must say I had a good time using them. I figured it was time someone violated what Orwell called 'the Geneva conventions of the mind' . . . a protocol that had kept journalism and non-fiction generally (and novels) in such a tedious bind for so long.

Wolfe says that he and other New Journalists – Gay Talese, Truman Capote, Terry Southern, Hunter S Thompson, Joan Didion – gradually learnt the techniques of social realism developed by novelists such as Fielding, Balzac and Dickens. They adopted such devices as realistic dialogue and scene-by-scene construction (telling the story by moving from scene to scene rather than by historical narrative).

Effectively they were claiming for journalism territory previously occupied by the novel – and repudiating the claim that journalism was somehow inferior to the novel. They were also helping to dispose of the idea that good writing is necessarily plain and simple.

Here's a snippet from a celebrated piece on the Kentucky Derby by gonzo journalist Hunter S Thompson, featuring the British cartoonist Ralph Steadman:

> I took the expressway out to the track, driving very fast and jumping the monster car back and forth between lanes, driving with a beer in one hand and my mind so muddled that I almost crushed a Volkswagen full of nuns when I swerved to catch the right exit. There was a slim chance, I thought, that I might be able to catch the ugly Britisher before he checked in.
>
> But Steadman was already in the press box when I got there, a bearded young Englishman wearing a tweed coat and HAF sunglasses. There was nothing particularly odd about him. No facial veins or clumps of bristly warts. I told him about the motel woman's description and he seemed puzzled. 'Don't let it bother you,' I said. 'Just keep in mind for the next few days that we're in Louisville, Kentucky. Not London. Not even New York. This is a weird place. You're lucky that mental defective at the motel didn't jerk a pistol out of the cash register and blow a big hole in you.' I laughed, but he looked worried.
> *Scanlan's Monthly*

'Gonzo', according to the dictionary, means 'bizarre, crazy, absurd'; is used about 'journalism of a subjective eccentric nature' – and, you might add, is certainly not politically correct. But, like the new journalism in general, this piece has life, colour and immediacy. Notice how specific it is: 'a Volkswagen full of nuns' rather than 'a carload of nuns'; 'a tweed coat and HAF sunglasses' rather than 'an overcoat and sunglasses'. Above all, it has the pace and rhythm of the spoken word. Clearly, the new journalism emphasises the continuity between speech and writing referred to above.

Earlier, the American journalist Studs Terkel developed a way of writing that took this link as far as it could be taken. His oral histories, such as *Working* and *The Good War*, are essentially edited first-person accounts. But as he once admitted, the art is in finding the natural storytellers to interview: 'You don't just bump into anyone.'

Blame the tape-recorder

In less talented hands writing that reproduces speech authentically can be repetitive, obscure, unstructured – in a word, unreadable. For the worst examples blame the tape-recorder and, in particular, the interviewing style known as Q&A. In what can be a travesty of journalism as an active, inquiring, interpretive process the interviewer's role seems to consist of turning the tape on and off, asking the odd question, then typing up the transcript with a minimum of editing – and in the laziest cases getting somebody else to do even that.

Here's an extract from a Q&A with a footballer, published in a (now defunct) monthly, *French News*. As you read it you can hear the original French in which the interview was conducted:

> TN: Are you thinking of coaching in the future?
> JPP: I'm thinking of it. It needs a lot of experience.
> TN: OK, but like many other high-level sportsmen you have got the best experience on the pitch.
> JPP: Managing a team is a different matter. I'm not ready yet.
> TN: You are a 'fighter' on the ground. Is this the sort of quality you would expect from your players?
> JPP: That's obviously what I would want from them.
> TN: Why not in Bordeaux?
> JPP: Why not indeed?

And so on – ad nauseam.

Write better than you talk

So reproducing speech as such can't be the answer to the style question. Indeed both Robert Gunning and John Whale ('Write the way you talk'/'Write as you speak') hedge more than a little when they go into detail.

The Gunning message turns into: 'Actually, we recommend that writers try to write better than they talk; to eliminate pauses, repetitions of words, and too many connectives. But the goal is to achieve a conversational tone.'

And Whale expands his slogan as follows:

> By this I mean that you should try to write as you would speak if you were talking at the top of your form, unhesitantly, in the idiom that best suited your theme and the occasion, and trusting your own ear.

To which you might object: but what if I have no top form to speak of, if I can't talk coherently and unhesitantly at the same time, if my ear is wooden and I don't feel able to trust it? Does it follow that I can't become a good writer?

Pushed to the limit, the Gunning–Whale argument fails. For there are certainly people who talk badly – hesitantly, repetitively, clumsily – but manage to write well. Some successful professional writers clearly do not write as they speak.

There is another, more general problem. Most people's speech has a looser grammar than their writing: sentences change direction without warning or are left unfinished; verbs don't agree with subjects; and so on. For most people, to follow the instruction 'write as you speak' would involve either slavishly copying the loose grammar of speech or having to go through the copy afterwards to tighten up the grammar.

'Write as you speak' turns out to be an overstatement of the obvious point that good written journalism has much in common with coherent speech. To put it another way, you don't really 'write as you speak', though to write well you may spend a lot of time and energy making it look as if you do.

Write with your ears

The simplest test of writing is certainly to read it out loud. You'll know immediately if sentences are too long: you won't have the puff to finish. You should be able to hear repetitions and clumsy constructions, too.

That is negative – a matter of avoiding mistakes. More positively, you should write with what is called cadence or rhythm. For example, write sentences that build to a powerful conclusion, as this one from Dickens does:

> It was my mother, cold and dead.

Here's a more elaborate example, also from Dickens:

> Annual income twenty pounds, annual expenditure nineteen nineteen six, result happiness. Annual income twenty pounds, annual expenditure twenty pounds ought and six, result misery.

A resignation note read simply:

> Hours too long, wages too low, life too short.

With his characteristic laconic style Julius Caesar reported to Rome:

> I came, I saw, I conquered.

And Dr Johnson produced this hard drinker's motto:

> Claret is the liquor for boys; port for men; but he who aspires to be a hero must drink brandy.

Writing in triplets like this works – the third element provides a punchline. Similarly, where there are two related points to make, try to make your sentence balance, as in this example from Hazlitt (in the *Times*):

> The love of liberty is the love of others; the love of power is the love of ourselves.

This is antithesis: contrasting two opposite points. It often uses the rhetorical device of repetition: here the word 'love' does not become 'affection' or 'passion' in the second clause; if it did, the sentence would lose its power.

The point about repetition is that it should be intentional, serving a similar function to rhyme in verse. On occasion it can run right through a section. Here's an extract from a feature published at the height of the President Clinton–Monica Lewinsky scandal in 1998:

> Let's review what we've learned so far. The president a liar? *Knew that.*
>
> The president a philanderer? *Knew that.*
>
> The president reckless in the satisfaction of his appetites? *Knew that.*
>
> The president would say anything and hurt anybody to get out of a mess? *Knew that.*
>
> Married men cheat? *Knew that.*
>
> Hillary isn't throwing Bill's stuff on the White House lawn because she is as committed to their repugnant arrangement as he is? *Knew that.*
>
> The president has the nerve to pick out a dress for a woman. *Didn't know that . . .*
> New York Times

'Knew that' runs like a chorus through the section – until we get to the punchline. Also note that 'the president' is repeated (except where Hillary comes into the story and 'Bill' is used).

There is a danger in writing with your ears: what might be called the Hiawatha effect – getting stuck in one soporific rhythm, as in:

By the shore of Gitche Gumee

By the shining Big-Sea-Water

Stood the wigwam of Nokomis

Daughter of the Moon, Nokomis . . .

Except to make a particular point (or to parody Longfellow) do not write like this: vary your rhythms.

Words and phrases

Words and phrases are the building blocks – and the flourishes – of writing. One single powerful word can transform a paragraph:

> Say what you like about the new ITV system that has arisen from the morass of the 1990 Broadcasting Act but you can't say it doesn't cater for minorities. GMTV, for example, caters for the brain-dead, a small but important proportion of the electorate whose needs have hitherto been addressed only by Rupert Murdoch.
> *Observer*

'Brain-dead' follows an innocuous-sounding sentence – which suddenly takes on a sharper meaning.

Next, here's a gossip writer in a London glossy commenting on objections by residents to a proposed memorial garden to Diana, Princess of Wales:

> It would be easy to deride the objectors for being cold-hearted but having seen the crowds, flowers and all those public tears, one can sympathise with Kensington residents who do not wish to walk out of their front door only to trip over some grieving wretch holding a bouquet.
> *London Portrait*

A fine example of 'writing for the reader': from the pompous misuse of 'deride' (the rest of us would say something like 'criticise' or 'condemn') to the strangulated 'one' (for 'you') this has the Kensington dialect to a tee. 'Grieving wretch' is superb.

A fixation with words whether read or heard can be put to good use. Here's a bit from an interview with Gerry Adams, who admits to being nervous before speaking in public and being interviewed:

> 'Yes. All interviews.' Gerry Adams fixes a steady gaze, and says, slowly and deliberately, 'I urinate a lot.'
>
> There is something very particular about the word 'urinate'. It is a term people seldom use unless they're talking to a doctor. The kind of person who chooses to tell you that they urinate when nervous is normally the

type to use words like 'tinkle' or 'waterworks'. But when Adams tells me that, he does so in the pared-down bald way characteristic of people who have endured extreme physical indignity; prisoners have it, and soldiers coming back from war.
Decca Aitkenhead, *Guardian*

Or how about this?

A recent trip to America has provided me with some splendid contemporary oxymorons to add to my already huge collection. I spotted 'airline food' before I'd even landed, and an airport menu furnished two more – 'jumbo shrimp' and 'this page intentionally left blank'. . . . My favourite was observed in Los Angeles: 'police protection'.
Victor Lewis-Smith, London *Evening Standard*

Original vivid phrases are worth their weight: they stop you having to rely on the cliché. Here's one from a report on the British bodybuilding championships: the heavyweights are described as plodding on with gigantic thighs so big they impede movement . . .

and buns so tight you could bounce brussels sprouts off them.
Observer

A vividly evoked picture: those huge bronzed, greased, muscular bottoms, elastically tight, and tiny green sprouts bouncing off them like squash balls – an attractively playful reaction to competitors who take themselves very seriously.

Successful phrases are often quirky, colourful, unexpected: they rely on contrast and conflict, the shock of the mismatched. For example, take a phrase and then – as though you'd landed on a snake during Snakes and Ladders – slide off somewhere surprising:

The British do not fear change. Only this morning a young man asked me for some.
Craig Brown parodying Tony Blair, *Daily Telegraph*

The only thing men get at present-giving time is bitterly disappointed.
Ms London

Or take a well-known phrase and turn it on its head:

He was an opera fanatic, and the sort of man who gives that species a good name.
Geoffrey Wheatcroft, *Opera*

Only the young die good.
Anon

Look for the unexpected, the vivid:

'She has Van Gogh's ear for music.'
Alex McGregor quoting Billy Wilder, *Probe*

Whoever writes his stuff deserves a place in Poets' Corner – as soon as possible.
Russell Davies, *Daily Telegraph*

Of a Serb militiaman manning a checkpoint in Bosnia:

If I die and go to hell, I expect him to be there at the gates.
Martin Bell, *Observer*

Of a character in a TV play:

A viper in peach silk and apricot satin
Richard Williams, *Guardian*

Overstatement can work – if it is vivid and specific. Here is the American journalist Dave Barry explaining 'Why Women Can't Play Baseball':

Because, faced with the choice of rescuing a drowning baby and catching a high fly ball, a woman wouldn't hesitate to save the baby, even if the game was tied and there were men on base.

Sentences and paragraphs

Start with the short sentence. That is: start by learning to write the short one, then practise adding longer ones to create contrast. Like this.

The impact of a short sentence is greater if it comes before or after a long one or several long ones. Here's a short sentence ending a paragraph:

It was on the morning of day three that I started to worry about George and Rose. We were tramping through the African bush, dutifully scanning the wilds for primeval monsters, when I suddenly noticed that George was wearing Bugs Bunny socks. *And Rose had floral shorts.* [My italics]

And here's the next par – starting with a short sentence:

Even worse, they were talking loudly. The great issue burning in their brilliant minds, as I tried to savour the incandescent glory of the African landscape, was this . . . [My italics]
Daily Telegraph

In both sentences and paragraphs the key points are the beginning and the end. As with the piece as a whole, you must get the reader's attention and then keep it. Try to begin and end with a strong word or phrase.

In general, above all with features, vary the length of your sentences. There is a place for a series of short ones – if you want to produce a breathless or staccato effect because what you're reporting is dramatic or terrible. Here, for example, is part of a quote from the fire brigade:

'The cottage is now completely gutted. Everything has gone. Only the walls are standing.'
Daily Telegraph

But there is no sense in writing a series of long sentences – unless your plan is to send the reader to sleep. Here, for example, is a paragraph of 71 words in just two sentences:

Ministers, and those they employ to whinge on their behalf, are now given to complaining that the media pay far too little attention to their achievements over the first year in office. It's an example of this Government's hypersensitivity, not to mention the ferocious rivalries within it, that I and other colleagues have been contacted by Cabinet Ministers and their functionaries over the past week with check-lists of their personal triumphs.
Observer

Political analysis seems to attract pompous and long-winded writing. In this case the sentences are long and complicated partly because the writer can't resist the aside, the parenthesis:

Ministers, and those they employ to whinge on their behalf, . . .

hypersensitivity, not to mention the ferocious rivalries within it, . . .

Complete sentences, like words and phrases, are often written in threes to produce a rhetorical effect:

Who were these people who sought to tell me what a good sunset is? Why were they invading my holiday? And how dare they defile my dusk?
Daily Telegraph

Figures of speech

Alliteration, metaphor, simile and the rest[2] are part of vivid, effective writing. But they can be overdone. The pun, for example, is a virus that gets into the computer systems of some tabloids.

Alliteration can be addictive. The local paper reporter who referred to 'Battersea's boxing brothers' (see page 16), which is straightforward, might not be able to resist the temptation of 'Clapham's cricketing cousins', which is clumsy and self-conscious.

And what about the *Telegraph* travel feature writer quoted above? Does his 'how dare they defile my dusk' work as a phrase? There's something awkward and forced in the combination of 'defile' and 'dusk'.

---

2 See *English for Journalists* for discussion of the common figures of speech.

Remember that alliteration – like other forms of repetition – can be unintentional. So sometimes you need to remove it from your copy to maintain an appropriate tone, to stop a serious piece sounding comic.

Tricks that don't work

As journalism has become more and more informal and colloquial, the mannerisms that might work in conversation – or even on radio – can look embarrassingly silly on the printed page. I've got no problem with slang, loose grammar, taboo words – what used to be called 'bad language' – when the context is right. I'm happy with 'And' and 'But' to start sentences. In columns and think pieces nothing beats a cunningly placed parenthesis (if only to keep the reader awake) . . . and so on.

But some 'tricks' just don't work. Here, in a piece in an upmarket newspaper about the BBC's Television Centre (and particularly the Blue Peter garden) being sold off, a sentence is fatally undermined by its first few words:

> Interestingly (always a bad start to a sentence), TV Centre was designed on the back of an envelope in a pub.

This is not interesting: it is bizarre. If 'interestingly' is a bad way of starting a sentence (not much doubt about that) why not forget it and start again? Is the reader supposed to think 'Well, if the writer knows it's lousy writing, that's all right then'? As I said, bizarre.

In general, beware of expressions like 'to coin a phrase'/'as the old joke has it'/'as they say'/'forgive the cliché' when you've decided that the only way to say something is to repeat a familiar formula. Forget the apology: just go ahead and do it.

The piece quoted above included another weird example of a trick that doesn't work:

> What will happen to the Blue Peter garden, which has existed at the back of the complex since Percy Thrower, pipe-smoking darling of TV gardening, turned the first sod (which is no way to talk about John Noakes) in 1832? Sorry I mean 1974.

I'm not referring to the 1832–1974 correction, which might be a bit clumsy but isn't worth commenting on. I mean 'sod'. Either the word is a friendly, informal word like bloke (in which case there's no objection to it) or it must mean what it originally meant – 'sodomite'. And that is certainly no way to talk about John Noakes, so why do it?

Too many buts

'But' is a powerful word. Like 'and', it has its place in journalism whether in the middle of sentences or at the beginning. But don't overdo it.

First, avoid the false 'but', often put in to revive a flagging sentence or paragraph. Second, avoid a succession of 'buts'. Even if some of them are 'however' or 'although', the effect is to leave the reader feeling giddy. For a 'but' changes the direction of the paragraph.

> The householder could, of course, search for the owner and arrange a deal. *But* tracing an owner is a long, laborious and frustrating task *although* local history may give some leads. Usually, it is when no-one comes forward with a paper title (title deeds), that householders technically squat. *But* it can be extremely frustrating . . . [My italics]
> *Ideal Home*

Too many 'buts'.

The importance of content

A word of caution to add to this emphasis on techniques and tricks: beware of putting colour into copy in an artificial way. Style, as was said early on in this chapter, is not a matter of adding embellishment to content. It is a matter of expressing content in a lively, vivid, pleasing way.

Faced with the (usually false) choice between style and content, many great stylists would in fact choose content. Here is that caustic wit Dorothy Parker, famous for her put-downs, reviewing the autobiography of the dancer Isadora Duncan:

> *My Life* . . . is a profoundly moving book. [Isadora Duncan] was no writer, God knows. Her book is badly written, abominably written. There are passages of almost idiotic naivety and there are passages of horrendously flowery verbiage. There are veritable Hampton Court mazes of sentences . . . There are plural pronouns airily relating to singular nouns but somehow the style of the book makes no matter. Out of this mess of prose come her hope, her passion, her suffering.
> *New Yorker*

Read, analyse, practise, polish

To develop your writing style, you need good models. We have tried in this book to provide some examples of the kind of journalistic writing we think you should read and try to emulate.

Look for well-written books by journalists – whether collected pieces or sustained reporting. *Homage to Catalonia* shows George Orwell at his best, reporting on the Spanish Civil War. Tom Wolfe's anthology *The New Journalism* has been quoted; there are good collections by the English interviewer Lynn Barber and the American ideologue P J O'Rourke; Ian Jack's *Before the Oil Ran Out* and Bill Bryson's *Made in America* are both worth reading. We also suggest that you read widely outside journalism: history, biography, novels. See 'Further reading' (page 187) for some suggestions.

Second, you need to go further than mere reading. You need to analyse the pieces you read and admire, and find out for yourself how they work. We suggest you follow the approach used in this book, naming and listing different types of intros and endings, for example. Does one of them contain a technique or trick you could use in your next piece?

Third – the most obvious point – you need all the practice you can get. With it, though, you need feedback.

If you work in the kind of office where copy just disappears into a black hole with never a word from anybody about how good or bad it is, you must try to get some reaction from other people – if not colleagues in the office, friends outside it.

Finally, polish: revise your pieces, and continue to revise them even after they've been published. Go back after a while and see how they could have been improved.

When you reread something you've written, play the sub who has to read it as a bored or hostile reader would. As we said earlier, try to read your copy out loud – ideally to a friend or colleague, otherwise to yourself. This way, you're likely to spot many of the errors and problems – repetition, awkward phrasing, obscurity. You could even read your copy into a tape-recorder, then play it back.

Always remember that you are writing for your reader not yourself. So be on the lookout for those fine phrases that seem brilliant at two in the morning but lose their shine the next day. If, as advised, you find yourself having to murder your darlings, they die in a good cause.

On the other hand, if you can make your writing lively, vivid, colloquial – and clear – you will serve your reader well and encourage them to keep coming back for more.

Glossary of terms used in journalism

Journalism is rich in jargon. Some of it comes from printing (book for magazine); or survives from the pre-computer age (spike for rejected copy); or is imported from the United States (clippings for cuttings). It is often punchy and graphic (ambush, bust, fireman). But if it crops up in copy (eg in stories about the media) the sub will usually have to change it (replace 'story' by 'report') or explain it (after 'chapel' insert 'office branch' in brackets). The obvious exception is in publications for journalists such as *Press Gazette* and the *Journalist*.

ABC: Audit Bureau of Circulations – source of independently verified circulation figures

ad: advertisement

add: extra copy to add to existing story

advance: 1 text of speech or statement issued to journalists beforehand; 2 expenses paid before a trip

advertorial: advertisement presented as editorial

agencies: news agencies, eg PA and Reuters

aggregation: process of combining data from various sources into a single new one

aggregator: organisation that collects and combines data from various sources

agony column: regular advice given on personal problems sent in by readers; hence agony aunt

algorithm: procedure or formula for solving a problem

ambush: journalists lying in wait for unsuspecting, unwilling interviewee

ampersand: & – symbol for 'and'

analytics: systematic analysis of data, particularly statistics

angle: particular approach to story, journalist's point of view in writing it

art editor: visual journalist responsible for design and layout of publication

artwork: illustrations (eg drawings, photographs) prepared for reproduction

ascender: the part of a lower-case letter (eg b and d) that sticks out above the x-height in a typeface

attribution: identifying the journalist's source of information or quote

author's (corrections, marks): proof corrections by writer of story

back number, issue: previous issue of publication

back of the book: second part of magazine (after the centre spread)

backbench, the: senior newspaper journalists who make key production decisions

backgrounder: explanatory feature to accompany news story

bad break: clumsy hyphenation at the end of a line

banner (headline): one in large type across front page

basket: where copy goes – once a physical basket, now a digital folder

bastard measure: type set to a width that is not standard for the page

beard: the space between a letter and the edge of the base on which it is designed

beat: American term for specialist area covered by reporter

bill(board): poster promoting edition of newspaper, usually highlighting main news story

black: duplicate of written story (from colour of carbon paper once used with typewriter)

bleed: (of an image) go beyond the type area to the edge of a page

blob: solid black circle used for display effect or to tabulate lists

blob par: extra paragraph introduced by blob

blog: regularly updated website or webpage consisting of separate entries (posts)

blow up: enlarge (part of) photograph

blown quote: another term for pull quote

blurb: displayed material promoting contents of another page or future issue

board: themed collection of images

body copy: the main text of a story, as opposed to page furniture

body type: the main typeface in which a story is set (as opposed to display)

bold: thick black type, used for emphasis

book: printer's (and so production journalist's) term for magazine

bookmark: record of a selected webpage or url so that user can easily return to selected site

bot: black on tone

box: copy enclosed by rules to give it emphasis and/or separate it from the main text

breaker: typographical device, eg crosshead, used to break up text on the page

brief: 1 short news item; 2 instruction to journalist on how to approach story

bring up: bring forward part of story to earlier position

broadsheet: large-format newspaper

bromide: photographic print

bullet (point): another term for blob

bureau: office of news agency or newspaper office in foreign country

business-to-business (b2b): current term for what were once called 'trade' magazines, ie those covering a business area, profession, craft or trade

bust: (of a headline) be too long for the space available

buy-up interview: exclusive bought by publication

byline: writer's name as it appears in print at the beginning of a story

c & lc: capital and lower-case letters

call out: another term for pull quote

calls (also check calls): routine phone calls made by reporters to organisations such as police and fire brigade to see if a story is breaking

camera-ready: (eg artwork) prepared for reproduction

caps: capital letters

caption: words used with a picture (usually underneath), identifying where necessary and relating it to the accompanying story

caption story: extension of picture caption into a self-contained story

cast off: estimate amount of printed matter copy would make

casual: journalist employed by the shift

catch(line): short word (not printed) identifying different elements of a story in the editorial process

centre: set type with equal space on either side

centre spread: middle opening of tabloid or magazine

chapel: office branch of media union (the shop steward is the father, FoC, or mother, MoC, of the chapel)

character: unit of measurement for type including letters, figures, punctuation marks and spaces

chequebook journalism: paying large sums for stories

chief sub: senior subeditor in charge of the others

churnalism: recycling, eg of press releases and pre-packaged material, without further research

city desk: financial section of British national newspaper (in the US the city desk covers home news)

classified advertising: small ads 'classified' by subject matter, grouped in a separate section

clippings/clips: American term for cuttings

close quotes: end of section in direct quotes

close up: reduce space between lines, words or characters

CMYK: cyan, magenta, yellow and black, the process (basic printing) colours

col: column

colour piece: news story written as feature with emphasis on journalist's reactions

colour sep(aration)s: method by which the four process colours (CMYK) are separated from a colour original

column: 1 standard vertical division of page; 2 regular feature by journalist often encouraged to be opinionated and/or entertaining

column rule: light rule between columns of type

conference: meeting of editorial staff to plan current/next issue

consumer magazines: the category includes specialist titles (eg *Angling Times*), women's magazines and those of general interest

contact sheet: photographer's sheet of small prints

contacts book: a journalist's list of contacts with details of phone, fax, email, etc

contents bill: *see* bill

controlled circulation: free distribution of specialist title to target readership by geography (free newspapers) or interest group (business-to-business magazines)

convergence: merging of media forms and platforms

copy: text of story

copy taster: *see* taster

copyright: right to reproduce original material

copytaker: telephone typist who takes down copy from reporter

corr: correspondent

correction: published statement correcting errors in story

correspondent: journalist covering specialist area, eg education

coverlines: selling copy on front cover

credit (line): name of photographer or illustrator as it appears in print next to their work

Cromalins: the Dupont system of glossy colour proofs

crop: cut (image) to size or for better effect

crosshead: line or lines, taken from the text, set bigger and bolder than the body type and inserted between paragraphs to liven up page

cut: shorten or delete copy

cut-out: illustration with background masked, painted or cut to make it stand out on the page

cuts: cuttings

cuttings: stories taken (originally cut) from newspapers and filed electronically under subject

cuttings job: story that is over-dependent on cuttings

dateline: place from which copy is filed

deadline: time story (or any part of it) is due

deck: originally one of a series of headlines stacked on top of each other; now usually used to mean one line of a headline

delayed drop: device in news story of delaying important facts for effect

delete: remove

descender: the part of a lower-case letter (eg g and j) that sticks out below the x-height in a typeface

desk: newspaper department, eg picture desk

deskman: American term for male subeditor

diary, the: list of news events to be covered; hence an off-diary story is one originated by the reporter

diary column: gossip column

direct input: transmission of copy direct from the journalist's keyboard to the computer for typesetting (as opposed to the old system in which compositors retyped copy)

disclaimer: statement explaining that a particular person or organisation was not the subject of a previously published story

display ads: ordinary (not 'classified') ads which appear throughout a publication

display type: type for headlines, etc

district reporter: one covering a particular area away from the main office

doorstepping: reporters lying in wait for (usually) celebrities outside their homes

double: a story published twice in the same issue of a publication

double-column: (of text, headline, illustration) across two columns

double (page) spread: two facing pages in a magazine, whether advertising or editorial

downtable subs: those other than the chief sub and deputies

drop cap, letter: outsize initial capital letter used to start story or section; it drops down alongside the text which is indented to accommodate it

drop quotes: outsize quotes used to mark quoted matter

dummy: 1 pre-publication edition of new publication used to sell advertising and experiment editorially; 2 blank version of publication, eg to show quality and weight of paper; 3 complete set of page proofs

edition: version of newspaper printed for particular circulation area or time

editor: senior journalist responsible for publication or section

editorial: 1 leading article expressing editorial opinion; 2 content that is not advertising

editor's conference: main planning meeting for next issue

em, en: units of measurement for type – the width of the two letters m and n

embargo: time before which an organisation supplying material, eg by press release, does not want it published

ends: the story ends here

EPD: electronic picture desk

EPS file: Encapsulated PostScript file

exclusive: claim by publication that it has a big story nobody else has

exes: journalists' out-of-pocket expenses

face: type design

facing matter: (of advertising) opposite editorial

facsimile: exact reproduction, as with electronic transmission of pages

favourite (to): to mark a tweet as a favourite

feature: article that goes beyond reporting of facts to explain and/or entertain; also used of any editorial matter that is not news or listings; hence feature writer, features editor

file: transmit copy

filler: short news item to fill space

fireman: traditional term for reporter sent to trouble spot when story breaks

fit: (of copy, etc) to occupy exactly the space available

flannel panel: magazine's address, contact information and list of staff

flash: brief urgent message from news agency

flatplan: page-by-page plan of issue

flip: (of picture) transpose left to right

flush left or right: (of type) having one consistent margin with the other ragged

fold, the: centre fold in a newspaper so that only the upper half of the paper ('above the fold') is visible at the point of sale

folio: page (number)

follow up: take published story as the starting point for an update

format: 1 size, shape or style of publication or section; 2 computer instruction; hence to format

fount (pronounced font and now often spelt that way): typeface

free(sheet): free newspaper

freebie: something useful or pleasant, often a trip, supplied free to journalists

freelance: self-employed journalist who sells material to various outlets

freelancer: American term for freelance

fudge: another term for stop press

full out: (of type) not indented

galley proof: typeset proof not yet made up into a page

gaming (the system): manipulating it for a desired outcome

gatefold: an extra page which folds out from a magazine

ghost writer: journalist writing on behalf of someone else, often by interviewing them; hence to ghost (eg a column)

gone to bed: passed for press so too late for corrections

grams per square metre (gsm; g/m2): the measure used to define the weight of paper

graphics: visual material, usually drawn

grid: design skeleton specifying (eg) number and width of columns

gutter: space between two facing pages; can also be used of space between columns

H & J: (of copy on screen) hyphenated and justified, so in the form in which it will be typeset

hack, hackette: jocular terms for journalist

hair space: thinnest space between typeset letters

half-tone: illustration broken into dots of varying sizes

handout: printed material, eg press release, distributed to journalists

hanging indent: copy set with first line of each paragraph full out and subsequent ones indented

hard copy: copy on paper, eg printout, rather than screen

hashtag: the # symbol used to mark key words or topics in social media

head, heading: headline

heavy: broadsheet newspaper

heavy type: thicker than standard

hold (over): keep material for future use

hot metal: old typesetting system in which type was cast from molten metal

house ad: publisher's advertisement in its own publication

house journal: publication for employees of a particular organisation

house style: the way a publication chooses to publish in matters of detail

imposition: arrangement of pages for printing

imprint: name and address of publisher and printer

in-house: inside a media organisation

in pro: in proportion (used of visual material to be reduced)

indent: set copy several characters in from left-hand margin

infographic: graphic visual representation of data

input: type copy into computer

insert: 1 extra copy to be included in existing story; 2 printed matter inserted in publication after printing and binding

intro: first paragraph of story; also used (confusingly) in some magazine offices to mean standfirst

ISDN: integrated services digital network – a means of transmitting editorial material between offices, to printers, etc

italics: italic (sloping) type

jackline: another word for widow

journo: jocular term for journalist

justified: type set with consistent margins

kern: reduce the space between characters in typeset copy

kicker: introductory part of caption or headline

kill: drop a story; hence kill fee for freelance whose commissioned story is not used

knocking copy: story written with negative angle

label: (of headline) without a verb

landscape: horizontal picture

layout: arrangement of body type, headlines, etc and illustrations on the page

lead: 1 main story on a page; 2 tip-off or idea for story (in the US the intro of a story is called the lead)

leader: leading article expressing editorial opinion

leader dots: three dots used to punctuate

leading (pronounced 'ledding'): space between lines (originally made by inserting blank slugs of lead between lines of type)

leg: column of typeset copy

legal: send material to be checked for legal problems, eg libel

legal kill: lawyer's instruction not to use

lensman: American term for male photographer

letter spacing: space between letters

libel: defamatory statement in permanent or broadcast form

lift: 1 use all or most of a story taken from one newspaper edition in the next; 2 steal a story from another media outlet and reproduce it with few changes

ligature: two or more joined letters

light face: type lighter than standard

linage (this spelling preferred to lineage): payment to freelances by the line; also refers to classified advertising without illustration

line drawing: drawing made up of black strokes

listicle: list-based article, eg '10 things you need to know about computers'

listings: lists of entertainment and other events with basic details

literal: typographical error

lobby, the: specialist group of political reporters covering parliament

local corr: local correspondent

logo: name, title or recognition word in particular design used on regular section or column; also used of magazine's front-page title

long-tail effect: publishing content online and keeping it available in an archive

lower case: ordinary letters (not caps)

make-up: assembly of type and illustrations on the page ready for reproduction

mark up: specify the typeface, size and width in which copy is to be set

masking: covering part of photograph for reproduction

masthead: publication's front-page title

measure: width of typesetting

medium type: between light and heavy

merchandising: details of stockists and prices in consumer features

metric: a system or standard of measurement

mf: more copy follows

model release: contract signed by photographic model authorising use of pictures

mono(chrome): printed in one colour, usually black

more: more copy follows

mug shot: photograph showing head (and sometimes shoulders)

must: copy that must appear, eg apology or correction

mutton: old name for an em

neg: photographic negative

news agency: supplier of news and features to media outlets

news desk: organising centre of newsroom

newsman: American term for male reporter

newsprint: standard paper on which newspapers are printed

newsroom: news reporters' room

nib: news in brief – short news item

night lawyer: barrister who reads newspaper proofs for legal problems

nose: intro of story; hence to renose – rewrite intro

NUJ: National Union of Journalists

nut: old name for an en; hence nutted, type indented one en

obit: obituary

off-diary: *see* diary, the

off-the-record: statements made to a journalist on the understanding that they will not be reported directly or attributed

on spec: uncommissioned (material submitted by freelance)

on-the-record: statements made to a journalist that can be reported and attributed

op-ed: feature page facing page with leading articles

open quotes: start of section in direct quotes

originals: photographs or other visual material for reproduction

orphan: first line of a paragraph at the foot of a page or column

out take: another term for pull quote

overlay: sheet of transparent paper laid over artwork with instructions on how to process it

overline: another word for strapline

overmatter: typeset material that does not fit the layout and must be cut

overprint: print over a previously printed background

PA: Press Association, Britain's national news agency

package: main feature plus sidebars

page furniture: displayed type, eg headlines, standfirsts and captions, used to project copy

page plan: editorial instructions for layout

page proof: proof of a made-up page

pagination: the number of pages in a publication; also a newspaper system's ability to make up pages

panel: another word for box

paparazzo/i: photographer(s) specialising in pursuing celebrities

par, para: paragraph

parallax scrolling: fluid scrolling that creates an illusion of depth with text overlaid on pictures or multimedia

paste-up: page layout pasted into position

patch: specialist area covered by reporter

pay-off: final twist or flourish in the last paragraph of a story

peg: reason for publishing feature at a particular time

photomontage: illustration created by combining several photographs

pic, pix: press photograph(s)

pica: unit of type measurement

pick-up (of photographs): those that already exist and can therefore be picked up by journalists covering a story

picture desk: organising centre of collection and editing of pictures

piece: article

plate: printing image carrier from which pages are printed

platform: computer's operating system

point: 1 full stop; 2 standard unit of type size

pool: group of reporters sharing information and releasing it to other media organisations

post: blog entry

PostScript: Adobe's page description language

PR(O): public relations (officer); hence someone performing a public relations role

press cuttings: *see* cuttings

press release: written announcement or promotional material by organisation sent to media outlets and individual journalists

profile: portrait in words of individual or organisation

proof: printout of part or whole of page so it can be checked and corrected

proofread: check proofs; hence proofreader

publisher: 1 publishing company; 2 individual in magazine publishing company with overall responsibility for title or group of titles

puff: story promoting person or organisation

pull: proof; to pull is to take a proof

pull (out) quote (blown quote, call out, out take): short extract from text set in larger type as part of page layout

pullout: separate section of publication that can be pulled out

pyramid: (usually inverted) conventional structure for news story with most important facts in intro

query: question mark

queue: collection of stories held in a computer

quote: verbatim quotation

quotes: quotation marks

ragged: (of type) with uneven margin

raised cap: outsize initial capital letter used to start story or section; it is raised above the text

range left or right: (of type) have one consistent margin with the other ragged

register: alignment of coloured inks on the printed page

rejig: rewrite copy, particularly in the light of later information

renose: rewrite intro of a story

repin: copy onto somebody else's board

reporter: gatherer and writer of news

repro house: company that processes colour pictures ready for printing

retainer: regular payment to local correspondent or freelance

retouch: alter photograph to emphasise particular feature

Reuters: international news agency

reverse indent: another term for hanging indent

reversed out: (type) printed in white on black or tinted background

revise: extra proof to check that corrections have been made

rewrite: write new version of story or section as opposed to subbing on copy

ring-round: story based on series of phone calls

river: white space running down a column of type, caused by space between words

roman: plain upright type

rough: sketch for layout

round-up: gathering of disparate elements for single story

RSI: repetitive strain injury, attributed to overuse and misuse of computer keyboard, mouse, etc

rule: line between columns or round illustrations

run: period of printing an edition or number of copies printed

run on: (of type) continue from one line, column or page to the next

running foot: title and issue date at the foot of the page

running head: title and issue date at the top of the page

running story: one that is constantly developing, over a newspaper's different editions or a number of days

running turns: pages with no paragraph breaks on first and last lines; also used of columns

rush: second most urgent message from news agency (after flash)

sans (serif): plain type (*see* serif) – this is an example of plain type

scaling (of pictures): calculating depth

schedule: 1 list of jobs for (eg) reporters; 2 publication's printing programme

scheme: make a plan of page layout

scoop: jocular word for exclusive

screamer: exclamation mark

screen: the number of dots per square inch of a half-tone

section: 1 separately folded part of newspaper; 2 complete printed sheet making up part of magazine

sell: another word for standfirst, often used in women's magazines

serif: decorative addition to type – this is an example of serif type

set and hold: typeset and keep for use later

setting: copy set in type

shareability: extent to which digital content is easily discovered and shared by others

shift: daily stint worked by staff journalists and casuals

shoot: a photographic session

shovelware: derogatory term for software notable for quantity rather than quality

shy: (of headline) too short for the space available

sidebar: subsidiary story or other material placed next to main story, usually in box

sidehead: subsidiary heading, set flush left

sign-off: writer's name as it appears in print at the end of a story

sketch: light-hearted account of events, especially parliamentary

slip: newspaper edition for particular area or event

small caps: capital letters in smaller size of the same typeface

snap: early summary by news agency of important story to come

snapper: jocular term for press photographer

snaps: press photographs

social media: websites and applications (apps) that enable users to create and share content or take part in networking

solid: (of type) set without extra leading

spike: where rejected copy goes (originally a metal spike)

splash: newspaper's main front-page story

splash sub: subeditor responsible for tabloid's front page

spoiler: attempt by newspaper to reduce impact of rival's exclusive by publishing similar story

spot colour: second colour (after black) used in printing publication

spread: two facing pages

s/s: same size

standfirst: introductory matter accompanying headline, particularly used in features

stet: ignore deletion or correction (Latin for 'let it stand')

stone: bench where pages were made up; hence stone sub – subeditor who makes final corrections and cuts on page proofs

stop press: small area on back page of newspaper left blank for late news in days of hot metal

story: article, especially news report

strap(line): subsidiary headline above main headline

Street, the: Fleet Street, where many newspapers once had their offices

stringer: local correspondent; freelance on contract to a news organisation

style: house style

style book/style sheet: where house style is recorded

sub: subeditor

subhead: subsidiary headline

subtitle: another word for standfirst

tab(loid): popular small-format newspaper such as the *Sun*

tagline: explanatory note under headline

take: section of copy for setting

take back: (on proof) take words back to previous line

take over: (on proof) take words forward to next line

taster: production journalist who checks and selects copy; also coverline

template: a document or file with a preset format

think piece: feature written to show and provoke thought

tie-in: story connected with the one next to it

tint: shaded area on which type can be printed

tip(-off): information supplied (and usually paid for) whether by freelance or member of the public

titlepiece: traditional term for name of magazine as it appears on the cover – now replaced by masthead and logo

TOT: triumph over tragedy, feature formula particularly popular in women's magazines

tracking: space between characters

trade names: product names (eg Hoover, Kleenex, Velcro)

tranny: transparency – photograph in film form

trans(pose): reverse order

turn: part of story continued on a later page

tweet: 140-character message sent via Twitter

Twitter: online social networking service

typeface: a complete range of type in a particular style, eg Times New Roman

typescale: measuring rule for type

typo: American term for typographical error

typography: craft of using type

u/lc: upper and lower case

underscore: underline

unj(ustified): text set flush left, ragged right

upper and lower case: mixture of capitals and ordinary letters

upper case: capital letters

url: uniform resource locator – the address for a file that is accessible on the internet

vignette: illustration whose edges gradually fade to nothing

vox pop: series of street interviews (Latin: *vox populi* – voice of the people)

weight: thickness or boldness of letters in a typeface

white space: area on page with no type or illustration

widow: single word or part of word at the end of a paragraph on a line by itself; originally the last line of a paragraph at the top of a page or column

wire: a means of transmitting copy by electronic signal; hence wire room

wob: white on black – type reversed out

wot: white on tone

x-height: height of the lower-case letters of a typeface (excluding ascenders and descenders)

Further reading

English usage and writing style

The best-known book on how to write good English, avoiding howlers, exists in four editions. The first one, *A Dictionary of Modern English*, edited by Henry (H W) Fowler, was published in 1926, and the second, edited by Ernest Gowers, in 1965. The third and fourth, edited by Robert Burchfield and Jeremy Butterfield respectively, are included in the list below.

Amis, Kingsley, *The King's English*, HarperCollins, 1997

Blamires, Harry, *Correcting your English*, Bloomsbury, 1996

Bryson, Bill, *Troublesome Words*, Viking, 2001

Burchfield, Robert, *The New Fowler's Modern English Usage* (third edition), Oxford University Press, 1996

Burridge, Kate, *Blooming English*, ABC Books for the Australian Broadcasting Corporation, 2002

Butterfield, Jeremy, *Fowler's Dictionary of Modern English Usage* (fourth edition), Oxford University Press, 2015

Cochrane, James, *Between You and I*, Icon, 2003

Dummett, Michael, *Grammar and Style for Examination Candidates and Others*, Duckworth, 1993

Evans, Harold, *Essential English for Journalists, Editors and Writers*, revised by Crawford Gillan, Pimlico, 2000

Gowers, Sir Ernest, *The Complete Plain Words* (second edition), revised by Sir Bruce Fraser, Pelican, 1977

Greenbaum, Sidney, and Whitcut, Janet, *Longman Guide to English Usage*, Penguin, 1996

Hicks, Wynford, *English for Journalists* (fourth edition), Routledge, 2013

—— *Quite Literally: Problem Words and How to Use Them*, Routledge, 2004

Humphrys, John, *Lost for Words*, Hodder, 2005

Lanham, Richard, *Style: An Anti-Textbook*, Philadelphia, PA: Paul Dry, 2007

Mayes, Ian, *Only Correct: The Best of Corrections & Clarifications*, Guardian, 2005

Partridge, Eric, *You Have a Point There*, Routledge, 1990

—— *Usage and Abusage* (third edition), revised by Janet Whitcut, Penguin, 1999
Pinker, Steven, *The Thinking Person's Guide to Writing in the 21st Century*, Allen Lane, 2014
Strunk, William, *The Elements of Style* (third edition), revised by E B White, Macmillan, 1979, also available free at www.bartleby.com/141/
Trask, R L, *Mind the Gaffe*, Penguin, 2001
Truss, Lynne, *Eats, Shoots & Leaves*, Profile, 2003
Waterhouse, Keith, *Waterhouse on Newspaper Style*, Viking, 1989
—— *English Our English*, Viking, 1991

House style

Austin, Tim (comp.) *The Times Style and Usage Guide*, Collins, 2003 (updated online edition: www.timesonline.co.uk)
The Economist Style Guide (eighth edition), Economist, 2003
Marsh, David, *Guardian Style*, Guardian, 2007 (updated online edition: www. guardian. co.uk)
Ritter, R M (ed. and comp.), *New Oxford Dictionary for Writers and Editors*, Oxford University Press, 2014

Print journalism

Adams, Sally, *Interviewing for Journalists*, Routledge
Frost, Chris, *Reporting for Journalists*, Routledge
Holmes, Tim, *Subediting and Production for Journalists*, Routledge
Keeble, Richard, *Ethics for Journalists*, Routledge
McNae's Essential Law for Journalists, latest edition, Butterworths
Mason, Peter, and Smith, Derrick, *Magazine Law*, Routledge

Non-fiction by journalists

This section includes collections and books about journalism. *Let Us Now Praise Famous Men* is classic reporting from the 1930s about three Alabama share-croppers – impoverished cotton farmers. *The Years with Ross* is a memoir of *New Yorker* editor Harold Ross.

Agee, James, and Evans, Walker, *Let Us Now Praise Famous Men*, Houghton Mifflin, 1991
Amis, Martin, *The Moronic Inferno*, Penguin, 1987
Barber, Lynn, *Demon Barber*, Viking, 1998
Bernstein, Carl, and Woodward, Bob, *All the President's Men*, Pocket Books, 1994

Bryson, Bill, *Made in America*, Minerva, 1995

Carter, Angela, *Nothing Sacred*, Virago, 1982

Coleman, Nick, and Hornby, Nick, *The Picador Book of Sports Writing*, Picador, 1997

Coward, Rosalind, *Speaking Personally: The Rise of Subjective and Confessional Journalism*, Palgrave Macmillan, 2013

Evans, Harold, *Good Times, Bad Times*, Phoenix, 1994

Harris, Robert, *Selling Hitler*, Arrow, 1996

Jack, Ian, *Before the Oil Ran Out*, Fontana, 1988

Malcolm, Janet, *The Journalist and the Murderer*, Granta Books, 2012

Marquez, Gabriel Garcia, *News of a Kidnapping*, Penguin, 2014

Marr, Andrew, *My Trade: A Short History of British Journalism*, Macmillan, 2004

Mitford, Jessica, *The Making of a Muckraker*, Quartet, 1980, out of print

O'Rourke, P J, *Holidays in Hell*, Picador, 1989

—— *Parliament of Whores*, Picador, 1992

Orwell, George, *The Collected Essays, Journalism and Letters of George Orwell*, vols I–IV, ed. Sonia Orwell and Ian Angus, Penguin, 1970

—— *Homage to Catalonia*, Penguin, 1989

Silvester, Christopher, ed., *The Penguin Book of Interviews*, Viking, 1993

—— *The Penguin Book of Columnists*, Viking, 1997

Terkel, Studs, *Working*, Penguin, 1985

Thurber, James, *The Years with Ross*, Penguin, 1963, out of print

Wolfe, Tom, and Johnson, E W, *The New Journalism*, Picador, 1990

Fiction

Allingham, Margery, *The Tiger in the Smoke*

Amis, Martin, *London Fields*, *Money*

Atwood, Margaret, *The Blind Assassin*

Boyd, William, *A Good Man in Africa*

Carey, Peter, *Oscar and Lucinda*, *Jack Maggs*

Le Carré, John, *The Spy Who Came in From the Cold*

Faulks, Sebastian, *Birdsong*

Greene, Graham, *The Power and the Glory*, *Brighton Rock*, *The Quiet American*

Hemingway, Ernest, just about everything – for the style rather than the content

Highsmith, Patricia, the Ripley books

Keane, Molly, *Good Behaviour*

Lurie, Alison, *The War Between the Tates*

McCullers, Carson, *The Member of the Wedding*, *The Heart is a Lonely Hunter*

Mailer, Norman, *The Naked and the Dead*

Mantel, Hilary, *Beyond Black*

Matar, Hisham, *In the Country of Men*

Maxwell, William, *So Long, See You Tomorrow*

Munro, Alice, *Runaway*

Proulx, Annie, *Close Range: Brokeback Mountain & Other Stories*
Steinbeck, John, *The Grapes of Wrath*, *Sweet Thursday*
Tyler, Anne, *Dinner at the Homesick Restaurant*
Vonnegut, Kurt, *Slaughterhouse-Five*
Waugh, Evelyn, *Decline and Fall*, *Scoop*
Wolfe, Tom, *Bonfire of the Vanities*

Index

Page numbers in italics refer to information in figures.